G000241647

VICTORIAN TABLE GLASS AND ORNAMENTS

VICTORIAN TABLE GLASS & ORNAMENTS

BARBARA MORRIS

BARRIE & JENKINS
COMMUNICA-EUROPA

First published in 1978 by
Barrie and Jenkins Limited
24 Highbury Crescent, London N5 1RX

ISBN 0 214 20551 7

Printed litho in Great Britain
by W & J Mackay Limited, Chatham

CONTENTS

ACKNOWLEDGEMENTS

IN the preparation of this book I have had help from many colleagues and friends and I should like to give special thanks to Hugh Wakefield (former Keeper of the Circulation Department of the Victoria and Albert Museum and an authority on Victorian glass) for reading the manuscript and offering both encouragement and advice. I should also like to offer my most sincere thanks to my former colleague Betty O'Looney (now Mrs Rowland Elzea) for freely making available all her notes and illustrations of Victorian glass, built up through many years of patient research.

My thanks are also due to the many museums, organisations and private owners, both at home and abroad, who have provided photographs, or allowed me to have photographed, objects in their collections, and given permission for their publication. The source of all these illustrations is individually acknowledged. I am especially grateful to Moira Walters of the Victoria & Albert Museum for taking some of the colour plates and many of the black and white photographs.

Finally I owe a special word of thanks to Dave Bowman for his persistent 'nagging' – over many years – without which this book might never have been completed.

LIST OF PLATES

INTRODUCTION

THE glassware produced in this country during the Victorian period presents an almost bewildering range of techniques and styles, and so no survey can hope to be fully comprehensive. The period saw a great expansion of the glass industry with an increasing use of mechanisation alongside the traditional processes of hand-manipulation and, in spite of competition from abroad, the opening up of new markets.

The removal of the excise duties on glass in 1845 undoubtedly gave a new impetus and a feeling of liberation to the industry, although the effect of the duties was not so disastrous as had been claimed. The financial effect at the luxury end of the trade had been very small, the proportion of taxation to the entire cost of the article representing only about two per cent. It was in those areas, such as window and bottle glass, where labour and skill did not form the chief element of cost that the tax hit hardest, about thirty per cent of the cost. In the best quality table glass, where the wages of the operatives far exceeded the basic cost of the materials, the tax element formed only a small proportion of the retail price. The real restraint on the industry had been the formal routine imposed by the excise regulations on the processes of manufacture. The removal of these restrictions gave more scope for experimentation, particularly in the development of coloured glass, in which Britain had hitherto lagged behind France and Central Europe. By the time of the Great Exhibition of 1851 the British manufacturers were able to show coloured glass that was worthy of comparison with that of their continental rivals. The repeal of the excise duties increased quantity as well as quality. Already in 1846, only a year after the taxes were removed, the *Art Union* was able to report a twenty per cent increase in the production of flint glass and a fifty per cent increase in the production of window glass.

This general increase in production, combined with the introduction of press-moulded glass with the consequent cheapness of manufacture, brought domestic glassware to the homes of all but the poorest section of the population. The emergence of a wealthy bourgeoisie meant a wider market for the more expensive styles of cut and engraved flint glass hitherto only available to the most affluent members of society, mainly the aristocracy and landed gentry. Towards the end of the Victorian period production had crystallised into three main streams catering for different social strata with widely differing tastes. At the top end of the scale were richly cut and engraved table glass and expensive novelties such as 'cameo' glass, for the high class trade and for export. Plainer, simpler glass, often historically based on earlier styles catered for those of aesthetic taste and for devotees of the Arts and Crafts movement. The third stream, the cheapest end of production, included pressed glass (sometimes in imitation of the current styles of cut glass, but often in entirely independent styles) and innumerable styles of fancy glass and novelties catering for the vast mass of the public.

Although, unlike the practice for silver or ceramics, very few extant examples of Victorian glass are marked with the name of the manufacturer or retailer, the periodicals of the time, notably the *Pottery Gazette and Glass Trades Review* (from 1877) [abbreviated under to *Pottery Gazette*] and the catalogues of the many international exhibitions enable one to plot the changing styles with some degree of certainty. Extant trade catalogues and surviving pattern books also enable glass to be attributed to individual manufacturers or at least provide a guideline to the approximate date of the piece in question. As with the other decorative and applied arts, no sooner had one manufacturer introduced a new pattern or a new style than others immediately sought to imitate it. The pattern books of the Stourbridge, London and Scottish glass-houses show a remarkable uniformity of style, and without documentary evidence it is often impossible to attribute a piece to a particular manufacturer with any degree of certainty.

The Patent Office Design Registers are one of the most reliable sources of dating and plotting the emergence of a new shape or method of decoration, but unfortunately only a minute proportion of the glass produced during the Victorian period was registered for design purposes, although new processes were often patented. Even if a decanter or similar article is found with a registration mark, this may often turn out to be registered not by the manufacturer but by the retailer, or even the importer. The design registers are most useful in the case of pressed glass. Sowerby & Company, of Gateshead-on-Tyne, for example, made no less than ninety-six separate registrations of their designs between 1872 and 1883, the individual registrations in some cases covering up to twenty-one different designs. In addition several of the leading makers of pressed glass had registered trade-marks which they impressed on most of their productions. There are also more extant catalogues of pressed glass than of the more expensive items. This is not surprising considering the volume of the trade and the fact that the catalogues were sent out to retailers, or agents abroad, and the goods ordered in bulk.

Attribution is especially difficult in the field of the cheaper fancy glass and novelties, some of it made in backyard cribs, not even in regular glass-houses. It is often almost impossible to determine whether a piece of this relatively cheap fancy glass is of English or Bohemian origin, so closely did the styles follow each other. At the cheaper end of the table glass ranges it is again often difficult to ascertain the country of origin, as a considerable number of British firms imported cheap glass from the Continent, notably from Belgium, which they proceeded to decorate by engraving, or, more frequently, by acid-etching. It is only by looking at, and above all handling, a vast quantity of nineteenth-century glass, that one gradually develops an instinctive recognition for the 'feel' of British glass.

CHAPTER 1

CUT GLASS

APSLEY Pellatt, in his *Explanatory Catalogue of Models and Specimens Illustrative of the Manufacture of Flint Glass Contributed to the Great Exhibition of all Nations* (London, 1851), describes the basic methods and the decorative aims of glass-cutting as:

'the forming of figures and patterns upon the plain surface of glass articles, by grinding away the glass with iron wheels and sand, soft stone and wood wheels follow to smooth and polish the figures formed by the iron wheels. The object to be obtained in cutting glass is to present such a surface to the rays of light that instead of them passing directly through the glass, they may be broken or refracted, so that 'the play of light', as it may be termed, is always on the surface. To effect this it is necessary that the lines forming the figure or the pattern upon the exterior of the glass be the reverse of the line of the *interior*, and that the indentations upon the surface, or the projections left by them, be such as to form angles. In the cutting called diamond or prism cutting, this object is at once obtained; the same effect is produced by fluting or flat cutting, because wherever two flat cuts meet, an angle is produced, forming with the line of the interior an imperfect prism; the broader the flat cuts, the more acute the angle, and consequently the greater the refraction of light, and as these cuts are made upon a circular surface, the broader the flats the more expensive.'

At the time of Queen Victoria's accession cut glass was the staple and most important production of the British glass-houses. The British cut glass of the early years of the nineteenth century, with its characteristic mitre- and diamond-cutting, enjoyed an international reputation and established a tradition which survives until the present day.

In the 1830s, however, before Victoria came to the throne, this so-called Regency style began to be replaced by a fashion for broad flute cutting, a style that first emerged about 1825. The typical Regency barrel-shaped decanter, ornamented with horizontal bands of diamond and mitre cutting, gave way to cylindrical decanters, decorated with vertical arrangements of broad hollow flutes, 'pillared' flutes, or simple flat vertical facets (Plate 1). The essential elements of this broad-fluted style can be seen in the pattern drawings of Samuel Millar, made at Waterford about 1830 (see M. S. Dudley Westropp, *Irish Glass*, 1920, p. 56, etc.)

According to the *Pottery Gazette* (March 1883, p. 269), in an article on 'Glass Cutting', the broad flute style originated in Birmingham, probably being first executed by a master glass-cutter called Morgan who worked for F. & C. Osler of Broad Street, Birmingham, the firm established by Thomas Osler in 1807. This was probably the Morgan listed in the Birmingham section of Pigot's *National Commercial*

1 Cylindrical form decanter cut in broad flutes. *c.* 1835. *Victoria & Albert Museum.*

2 Claret jug cut in broad facets. *c.* 1840. h. 12¾ in. *Victoria & Albert Museum.*

3 Waisted bell-shape decanter cut in the broad flute style. *c.* 1845. h. $12^1/_2$ in. *Victoria & Albert Museum*.

Directory for 1835 under glass-cutters and manufacturers as Pitt and Morgan, Baskerville House. Another Birmingham glass-cutter, John Gold, was also prominent in the development of this style. In 1832, when he was a master cutter at the Aetna Glass Works of George Joseph Green, Gold patented a machine for broad flute cutting. The 1835 list of glass-cutters and manufacturers lists John Gold at Steam Mills, Charlotte Street, and describes him as 'sole patentee of an improved method of glass cutting'. In spite of this, the machine does not seem to have been a commercial success, although John Gold was considered as among the most able and talented designers and executants of cut glass. Morgan and Gold are mentioned again in relation to the broad flute style in two further articles in the *Pottery Gazette* (1884, p. 73 and 1889, p. 238). The 1884 article states that John Gold was succeeded by a Mr Bedford, as Bedford and Geddis, glass-cutters. It is possible that this Mr Bedford was connected with Sarah Bedford & Company, who appear in an 1830 directory of Birmingham as flint- and cut-glass manufacturers of 16 New Street. Yet another prominent Birmingham glass-cutter of the period was Benjamin Price, who, in spite of being blind, conducted

4 Water jug of cut glass with mould-blown frosted medallions of Shakespeare, Milton, Burns and Byron. *c.* 1840. Possibly made by F. & C. Osler of Birmingham or John Ford of Edinburgh. h. 8 in. *Victoria & Albert Museum.*

his glass-cutting business in the Bull Ring with great success. His premises were burnt down in the Chartist riots of 1852.

At this time, in the 1830s, Birmingham was generally held to take the lead in glass-cutting, although the city by no means held a monopoly of the trade. In London, Hancock & Rixons, and James Green (later James Green and Nephew) were prominent, but they still specialised in diamond-cutting, for which there was a steady demand, particularly for the American market. Diamond-cutting was also widely practised in the leading glass-houses in Stourbridge. By 1840, however, the broad flute style was in general use. In a catalogue of Apsley Pellatt and Co. of about 1842, the broad flute style is well represented in decanters, claret jugs, wine glasses, finger bowls, custard cups, pickle jars, etc., although there are a number of hangovers from earlier Regency styles.

One of the most elegant forms of the broad flute style was a simple decanter with a slightly swelling body narrowing towards a single neck ring, cut in eight broad flutes, with a spire stopper. These decanters were made both in clear crystal and in green glass. The flutes were sometimes left plain, but often the alternate flutes were engraved with a running vine pattern (see Plate 5). The alternate flutes were also sometimes stained yellow or ruby. Mushroom and flattened stoppers were also used with the broad flute style.

Broad flute cutting was also applied to claret jugs (Plate 2), liquor bottles, water carafes and pickle jars, as well as to smaller articles such as finger bowls, wine-glass coolers, tumblers, wine glasses and goblets. The tumblers were cut with six, eight or twelve flutes round, sometimes with a split cut between the flutes. The base of the bowl of a wine glass or goblet was similarly cut and the wine-glass bowls were cup-, bell- or bucket-shaped, or conical. If the bowl was cut, the stem was usually cut as well. The cut stems presented considerable variety with cut pedestal stems, inverted balusters, and six fluted stems with a central knop cut in diamond facets. A feature of the broad flute style was continuous fluting flowing from the stem into the bowl and a tall, trumpet-shaped glass was especially characteristic.

The broad flute style was essentially international, a style that had some affinity with the Biedermeier, when the fashion for densely coloured glass with a marble-like appearance called for a new kind of cutting, in plain broad facets.

5 Spirit decanter and stopper cut in broad flutes with engraved decoration. *c*. 1840. h. $11^{5}/_{8}$ in. *Private collection.*

Parallel with the fashion for broad flute cutting was pillar cutting, in which the flutes were convex instead of concave or flat. Pillar cutting was used extensively on decanters and claret jugs. The pillars were sometimes further cut with 'printies' or olives, particularly in the Stourbridge glass-works such as Webb's and Richardson's. A typical example, said to have been shown at the 1851 Exhibition, is illustrated in Plate 9.

In the 1840s, the Gothic influence led to a marked fashion for arched motifs, patterns which recalled the tracery of Gothic church windows and had the strong vertical emphasis associated with the broad flute style. The arched panels, which formed a sort of arcading round the body of the vessel, might be left plain or filled in with mitre- or diamond-cutting. In the case of bowls or dishes the spaces between the tops of the Gothic arches might be filled in with fan scallops or 'shell' motifs as they were often called.

Apart from the Gothic style, the various revived historical styles had little direct influence on cut glass as the technique itself imposed certain limitations. The revived rococo style, particularly evident in both the shapes and decoration of ceramics and silver, was hardly suitable for heavy cut glass. However, the prevailing feeling for

6 Honey jar and cover with cut decoration in the style prevalent between the years 1845 and 1855.
Victoria & Albert Museum.

curved and asymetrical motifs did have some slight influence during the later 1840s and 1850s. W. H., B. & J. Richardson of Stourbridge were prominent in this respect, producing services, dishes, celery vases and other items in which panels of fine diamond-cutting were placed between diagonally curving cut ribs, or arranged in coiling patterns, the edges of the dishes being fan- or shell-scalloped. These styles, however, were not particularly new, being extensions and variations of patterns already current in the cut glass of the early nineteenth century.

The 1840s and 1850s saw a fashion for a 'roughed' surface to the whole or part of the surface of vessels which were to be decorated by cutting. This style was especially popular for water jugs and goblets, celeries, sugar and finger bowls, the polished cut motifs contrasting with the matt surface of the roughened area. Pear-shaped water jugs, with scalloped tops and high flaring lips, and seven or nine flutes round, were roughed all over with polished cut splits between the flutes. Others were more elaborately decorated with a series of horizontal festoons on each flute. Simple 'olives', circular balls, or splits and hollows, were also cut against the roughed surface. A simple all-over diaper pattern of eight-pointed cut stars was also

7 Water jug and two goblets with intaglio cut leaf decoration with roughed finish. *c.* 1848–50. Jug. h. 10½ in. *Photograph Victoria & Albert Museum.*

common. Large cup-bowled, or inverted bell-shaped goblets were often decorated in this way, but the top of the goblet was always left smooth and polished, as the roughened surface would have made drinking unpleasant. A particular fashion that arose in the mid-1840s was the placing of roughened leaf motifs round the base of jugs and decanters, the bowls of wine glasses, goblets and finger bowls, and the foot and rims of tazzas or comports (Plates 7, 8). The outline of the leaf was defined by thin 'edge-cutting' and the veins were similarly indicated. The simple leaf pattern was sometimes elaborated by the introduction of bulrushes or lilies-of-the-valley between the leaves. Greek key patterns, or more elaborate classical scrolls, or simple stylised flowers were also employed for cut patterns against the roughened background. All these styles were much imitated in the pressed glass of the late 1850s and 1860s (see Chapter 11).

A 'fuschia' pattern decanter and wine glass by Richardson's (illustrated in the *Journal of Design* vol. I, 1849, p. 51), shows an extension of the leaf motif, for the decanter itself has been made in the shape of the pendant fuschia blossom, the calyx and petals defined by roughening, with the stamens engraved between the petals. This is one of relatively few examples in glass of the imitative naturalism of the 1840s which was much more apparent in ceramics and silver.

In 1845, after many years of agitation, the excise duty on glass was finally removed. Although the ill effects of the tax were perhaps not so severe as had been claimed, being most restrictive on window rather than table glass, the removal of the excise duty had a liberating effect and gave a new impetus to the industry. One effect was to revive an interest in deep mitre-cutting, which involved making much thicker and heavier vessels. The result was often clumsy and awkward, the basic shape being distorted by deep, over-elaborate cutting, and the form being lost in a mass of detail. This was particularly apparent in some of the glass shown at the Great Exhibition of 1851. The *Art Journal Illustrated Catalogue*, for example, gives some engravings of three decanters by Lloyd and Summerfield of Birmingham which are described as being of 'the purest cut crystal, ornamented with much novelty of design, the forms whereof [sic] being in very bold relief, bring out the colour of the glass in an exceedingly brilliant style'. The first decanter has a rosette in an onion-shaped deep cut panel, which is repeated four times round the body, and the neck is heavily cut. The second has a more formal pattern built round a circular disc, again repeated four times, and the third a sort of Catherine-wheel motif, with the neck cut in irregular facets.

They also justify the condemnations of Somers Clarke in his contribution on 'Table Glass' to the *Arts and Crafts Essays* (London 1893) where he states that the material was produced in 'mere lumps, cut and tormented into a thousand surfaces, suggesting that the work was made from the solid', and that the mid-nineteenth-century decanter was 'a massive lump of mis-shapen material better suited to the purpose of braining a burglar than decorating a table'. These 'monstrosities' were all too common in the mid-nineteenth century. At the 1851 Exhibition Richardson's showed a decanter the globular body of which was deeply cut like a prickly pineapple, with stopper to match, and in others the necks were cut with so many facets that the shape was almost lost.

In the 1860s and 1870s the fashion for thinly blown glass, which was more suited to engraved or etched decoration, led to a decline in cutting with few innovations in style, although cut glass continued to be produced, especially for export. Most of the cutting was fairly rudimentary, often with some simple cutting combined with engraved decoration. The successful imitation of cut glass by

8 Comport with intaglio cut leaf decoration and roughed finish. Probably made by Molineaux Webb & Co., Manchester. *c.* 1850. diam. $9^3/_4$ in. *Private collection.*

pressing, combined with the intellectual revolt against it, led by writers such as Ruskin and Morris and others connected with the aesthetic movement, contributed to the decline.

In the next decade the reaction set in and the 1880s saw a revival of glass-cutting with the introduction of what is known as 'brilliant' cutting. On 1 February 1882 the *Pottery Gazette* was to claim that 'it is evident that the *plain era* in glass is dying out; plain wines and clarets, as well as plain decanters are doomed, and the brilliant period is coming in again. At least let us hope that aestheticism is on the wane as far as glass is concerned, for it means no labour and as little trade, and certainly very little taste'.

During the 1880s and 1890s elaborate cut glass, with its rich and opulent effect, adorned the dinner tables and sideboards of the wealthy middle and upper classes. Those who favoured the Arts and Crafts movement still eschewed it and its appeal was to more conservative tastes, which saw it as the acme of refinement and elegance. The manufacturers generally welcomed the revival and referred to it as the 'old legitimate trade' (*Pottery Gazette*, 1889, p. 791). Indeed there was a conscious revival of earlier styles. A number of firms,

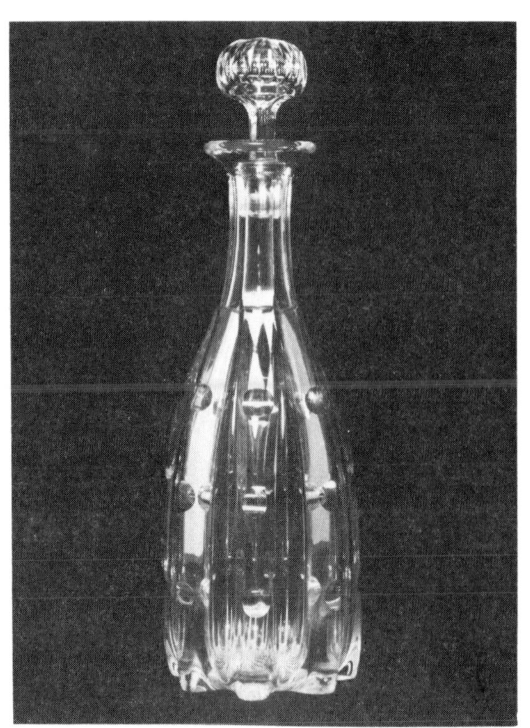

9 Pillar-moulded decanter with cut decoration made by W. H., B. & J. Richardson, Stourbridge. 1850–1. From a Richardson family collection, traditionally said to have been shown at the Great Exhibition of 1851. h. 11¾ in. *Victoria & Albert Museum.*

10 Decanter and stopper with cut decoration made by W. H., B & J. Richardson, Stourbridge. 1850–1. From a Richardson family collection, traditionally said to have been shown at the Great Exhibition of 1851. h. 12½ in. *Victoria & Albert Museum.*

notably Richardson's, applied deep rich cutting to some reproductions of old shapes, especially those from the times of George IV, including three-ringed decanters, water jugs and bucket-shaped goblets.

As James O'Fallon pointed out in an article on glass cutting, in the *Art Journal* of 1885, by the very nature of its technique cut glass offered less scope for imaginative design than other forms of decorated glass:

> Glass cutting does not offer such a wide field for inventive genius and artistically finished work as does glass engraving and carving; but it can be immensely improved, and brought more into harmony with educated taste. Diaper all over the body of a jug, decanter or the bowl of a wine glass, facet with facet, prism with prism alike, is what the glass-cutter in general likes to do. His wheel, while cutting a line, lends itself freely to continuing it as far as the vessel allows, up or down, or horizontally, or diagonally. His natural tendency is to repeat this operation by crossing and recrossing the line. The result is manifest: his patterns are too geometrical, and lack variety.

1 'Brilliant' cut decanter and stopper made by tevens & Williams, Brierley Hill. 1887. In the ossession of the makers. h. 14 in. *Photograph Victoria & Albert Museum.*

12 'Brilliant' cut claret jug engraved with the arms of the King of Italy. Made by F. & C. Osler of Birmingham. *c.* 1893. h. 14¼ in. *Peter A. G. Osler. Photograph Victoria & Albert Museum.*

This tendency was certainly apparent in the 1880s as far as articles such as the square-sided whisky decanters and spherical scent or toilet water bottles of the late Victorian period were concerned. These were invariably cut all over with octagon, diamond or hobnail patterns with the inevitable spherical lapidary stopper, which harmonised with the brilliant-cut body. Even so, during the period of brilliant cutting, there was a great deal of variety in the way the patterns were arranged although based on various all-over diapers, and many other motifs were introduced into the designs which achieved an extraordinary degree of elaboration.

Cut-glass decanters, claret jugs and flower vases appeared in wide variety, with tall, slim shapes predominating, usually set on a spreading foot with a 24-point star cut on the underside (Plates 11, 12). Elongated forms with a broad base rising to a narrow neck were also found, and a thistle shape, with the calyx imitated by diamond-cutting was popular for glasses, and, in inverted form, for decanters with a thistle-like lapidary stopper. Technical improvements led to greater control of the cutting, making it possible to produce much more complex articles such as baskets and elaborately shaped flower vases. An offshoot of the fashion for the 'Brilliant' cut glass was an increased production of exclusive patterns for silversmiths, and articles such as heavy cut-glass salad bowls with silver rims, claret jugs and spirit decanters, biscuit barrels, cruets, toilet sets, etc., which were produced in great quantities. For the collector these have the distinct advantage that they can be precisely dated by the hallmarks on the silver.

CHAPTER 2

COLOURED AND SILVERED GLASS

COLOURED glass was not made in England in any substantial quantities until the middle of the nineteenth century, the manufacturers tending to concentrate on the production of lead crystal glass, on which the reputation of the British glass industry rested. The Bohemian glass-houses were pre-eminent in the field of coloured glass, especially cased glass, and in the late 1830s and 1840s the British glass manufacturers began to meet this competition. Whereas the British manufacturers at no time sought to rival the heavily coloured opaque and marble-like glass known as 'hyalith' or 'lithyalin' which was characteristic of the Biedermeier period, from 1835 onwards a number of firms began to produce coloured and layered glass, as well as opaline, and also to apply surface stains, both ruby red, derived from copper, and a yellowish brown derived from silver. A mid-1830s pattern book of Stevens and Williams contains many examples of coloured glass, mostly cased, as an alternative to the colourless lead crystal cut glass. Similarly, in the 1830s, Thomas Hawkes of Dudley were making 'gold-enamel' wares and by the 1840s most of the Stourbridge firms were employing surface staining in conjunction with the broad flute style of cutting. The use of colour became much more widespread with the repeal of the excise duty in 1845.

Pre-eminent in the development of coloured glass was the Stourbridge firm of W. H., B. & J. Richardson, dominated by Benjamin Richardson, who later in the century came to be known as 'the father of the glass trade' (*Pottery Gazette*, 1888, p. 50), and it was said that 'what Josiah Wedgwood did for the pottery trade, Benjamin

Richardson did for the glass trade' (*Pottery Gazette*, 1897, p. 475). By 1845 the *Art Union* was to remark that in Richardson's coloured glass there were laudable attempts to rival the produce of Bohemia and that in a cased and cut scent bottle 'the blue is more perfect than any hitherto produced in this country. Their greens and crimsons are also decidedly good; in fact they nearly approach in excellence the best of our foreign importations.' At the Birmingham Exhibition of 1849 Richardson's, George Bacchus & Sons, and Rice Harris all exhibited coloured glass and in reviewing the exhibits the *Art Journal* commented that 'we have almost every variety of colour and in most instances the tints rival in beauty those which we have so long admired.'

Richardson's seem to have made a speciality of an almost opaque apple-green glass which they used for a wide variety of articles including covered butter dishes and stands, scent bottles and comports, mostly with turned-over rims decorated with scallops and gilding. Sometimes green and white opaline were combined as in a comport of white opaline with a scalloped edge of green and a white

13 Jug and goblet of ruby glass cased on crystal with the decoration cut and engraved through the coloured layer. *c.* 1850. Jug h. 12½ in. *Brierley Hill Collection.*

vase with a green globular base. Opaline green (or, less frequently, opaline blue) snakes were also used as decoration.

The official catalogue of the Great Exhibition of 1851 shows that by that time a considerable quantity of coloured glass was being made in this country. Ruby glass was possibly the most common and many firms showed epergnes (combining a fruit bowl with a central flower vase), finger bowls, decanters, liqueur bottles, hock glasses and vases, made of ruby glass. Davis, Greathead & Green of Stourbridge, apart from the more common opaline, listed vases and scent bottles, many of them cut, coated, gilded or painted in enamel colours, in a wide range of colours – ruby, Oriental blue, chrysoprase, turquoise, black, rose colour, opal-coated blue, cornelian, mazareen blue and topaz. George Bacchus & Sons had a similar range of colours including a 'Pomona' or apple green similar to that favoured by Richardson's, and much the same variety occurs in Rice Harris's entry with the addition of brown and purple. Apsley Pellatt showed yellow, blue, purple, rose and ruby, topaz and emerald green, and gave details of the methods used to produce the different

14 Three examples of silvered glass acquired in 1851 from the Silvered Glass Company. The tall goblet is marked 'E. Varnish & Co.', and the salt cellar of ruby layered glass with cut decoration and the goblet with engraved vines are both marked 'Hale Thomson's Patent'. h. $8^7/_8$ in., 3 in. and 4 in. *Conservatoire National des Arts et Métiers, Paris.*

15 Standing bowl of ruby glass layered with opaque white glass, cut in 'Gothic' style. Mid-19th century. h. $5^1/_2$ in. *Victoria & Albert Museum.*

colours employing the oxides and carbonates of various metals, including copper, iron, gold and uranium, as well as cobalt and manganese.

The exact nature of some of these colours, which were often given somewhat arbitrary ephemeral names, is not always clear, but Oriental blue was probably a deep cobalt akin to the blue on Chinese blue and white porcelain and mazareen blue a somewhat deeper shade. As well as actual coloured glass, that is, glass coloured all through the metal, coloured stains were also used. These stains, which were no more than a thin wash of colour on the surface, were confined to red and yellow, produced by the use of gold and silver. In addition to the transparent colours, which were used in the same way as the colourless flint glass, a number of semi-transparent colours, akin to the near-white opal or opaline in density, were employed, an apple green or turquoise blue being most favoured.

The extensive range of coloured glasses was often combined with flint or opaline glass. The use of colour in 'cased' or layered glassware, which features extensively in the continental glass of the Biedermeier period, occurs to a limited extent in England from the mid-1830s but it was not until after the repeal of excise duties in 1845 that cased glass became widespread in this country. The method used to produce cased glass was relatively simple. A gather of molten glass, which was to form the body of the vessel, was put into a prepared hollowed case of another colour and the two layers were then fused or welded together by heat. The mass thus formed was then blown into the required shape. This basic process could be used to produce two, three, or even four layers of different-coloured glass. Normally the body of the vessel was of colourless glass with an outer layer of one or more colours, but, alternatively, a layer of opaque white glass might be used between two coloured transparent layers. Most of this cased glass was decorated by cutting so that the original body was exposed through the various layers in the areas where it was cut. This technique was widely used for decanters and spirit bottles, jugs and goblets (Plate 13), comports and bowls, and especially for smaller articles such as scent and toilet water bottles. Sometimes conventional mitre-cutting was employed, the George Bacchus & Sons decanter shown in Plate 17 being a particularly sophisticated example. The Gothic style was much favoured for the cutting of cased glass with cusped outlines giving the effect of a traceried window (Plate 15), but shapes of leaves and flowers were also used. In some instances the glass was further decorated by enamelling and gilding (Plate 18), but this was less common in England than in Bohemia. Layering was also used as a coloured ground for engraving which would cut down to expose the colourless glass below, as in a fine goblet designed by W. J. Muckley shown by Richardson's at the 1851 Exhibition and now in the Council House Collection at Stourbridge. The thick ruby casing on this goblet gave much more scope to the engraver than the more usual ruby or yellow stain where the engraving was of necessity fairly shallow.

A particularly interesting novelty, which enjoyed a brief but successful vogue, was silvered glass. The main patent was taken out on 19 August 1849, by Frederick Hale Thomson and Edward Varnish and the technique consisted in precipitating silver over the interior surface of a double-walled vessel by means of a solution of silver nitrate and glucose, which was then poured off, leaving a deposit of silver, and the opening sealed against the atmosphere. The

Art Journal (1850 p. 265), in a piece entitled 'Patent Glass Silvering', described the patent in some detail:

> Mr Hale Thomson has recently introduced a new and beautiful process for coating glass surfaces with a deposit of pure silver . . . the brilliancy is greater, and the colour warmer and more agreeable than that of the amalgam of tin and quicksilver with which our ordinary-looking glasses are coated, and so it is applicable to every variety of curved surface, the inside of the smallest glass tube being silvered with the same facility as a flat surface: coloured glass thus coated adds its colour to the metallic brilliancy of the silver seen through it; and thus the effect of gold, bronze and steel can be produced in addition to the many harmonious combinations of silver and coloured glass, which the cutting and engraving of surfaces flashed with a thin layer of coloured glass will produce. The silver is protected from tarnishing by the glass to which it adheres and at its outer surface by a preservative coating

16 Footed bowl in silvered glass, the base marked 'E. VARNISH & CO. LONDON. PATENT'. *c.* 1850. h. 7 in. *Sotheby's Belgravia.*

17 Decanter and stopper of ruby glass overlaid with opaque white glass and spirally cut in diamonds. Made by George Bacchus & Sons, Birmingham. *c.* 1850. h. 12½ in. *Victoria & Albert Museum.*

of cement . . . Its application to ornamental table glass, to epergnes, toilet bottles, flower vases, for instance, are endless. . . . A brilliant and beautiful colour is produced of different tints even in the same goblet, which may have all the variety and beauty of the Bohemian glass, with the extra brilliancy of metallic tints, and a totally different colour for the interior to that used in the exterior of the articles fabricated.

Sometimes the articles were fashioned from clear, colourless glass, giving the appearance of a silver vessel (Plate 16), but often an additional casing of coloured glass – usually ruby, blue, green or purple – was placed on the vessel, and then cut or engraved to expose

18 Vase of pale ruby glass, with opaque white glass overlay partially cut away and gilt. Probably made by W. H., B. & J. Richardson, Stourbridge. *c.* 1850. h. 12 in. *Victoria & Albert Museum.*

the silvered glass (Plate 14). Gothic patterns and other geometric motifs, as in the normal cased glass, or running patterns of flowers and leaves were employed. A goblet made by this process, now at Osborne House in the Isle of Wight, has medallion heads of Queen Victoria and Prince Albert, and the Royal Coat of Arms. Goblets, standing bowls, vases, inkwells and paperweights were all made in this technique, but the process precluded any great refinement or complexity of shape and the attraction of the glass lies in its surface glitter.

The glass patented by Frederick Hale Thomson and Edward Varnish was probably made by James Powell & Sons of Whitefriars. Edward Varnish & Co., of 48 Berners Street appear to have been retailers rather than manufacturers, and showed a group of the patent silvered glass at the Great Exhibition of 1851, describing themselves as 'Patentees & Proprietors'. Joseph George Green (later Green & Nephew) of St James's St., Piccadilly showed an ormolu chandelier, in Elizabethan style, at the 1851 Exhibition, which they described as 'fitted with glass, silvered by Varnish & Co's patent'.

Other individuals, probably retailers, were also associated with the patent, as various wordings are found on the base of the vessels. 'E.VARNISH & CO/ PATENT/ LONDON' is most frequently found, but 'HALE THOMSON'S PATENT LONDON' and 'W.LUND /PATENT/ LONDON' have also been found on a number of objects. Similar silvered glass was made in Bohemia, including figures, but the English examples are generally more expertly made and finished.

In August 1850 Frederick Hale Thomson took out another patent for silvering glass, this time in conjunction with Thomas Robert Mellish, but this seems to have been confined to various methods of decorating, by cutting, staining and silvering flat surfaces such as mirror surrounds. Similarly William Kidd of Poland Street evolved a method of decorating glass by engraving the underside of mirrors with borders of flowers, fruit, etc., prior to silvering. He gave the name 'embroidered glass' to the process, which was considered suitable for the interior of ladies' work-boxes, the tops of ornamental tables, finger plates, etc. In describing Kidd's method the *Art Journal* (1850, p. 202) stated 'it was suggested that the process could also be applied to the ornamenting of goblets, decanters, wine glasses, etc.', but it is not known whether William Kidd's method, by which the engraved patterns appeared as if in relief on the surface of the glass, was ever used for the decoration of table glass.

Another method of silvering glass, known as 'Drayton's process', was also introduced about 1850. The *Art Journal* (1 February 1853, p. 39) described it as 'an ingenious mode of silvering glass; . . . possessing great facilities over the old mode, it has enabled manufacturers to astonish the world with flagons, goblets, ewers, etc., having the appearance of silver but wrought, where the surface was not covered with frosted ornaments, to a most remarkable brilliancy; and this at a price for which the like articles could not be produced even in copper. The new manufacture has, we believe, found ready purchasers, and is likely to become a permanent branch of "Decorative Art"'.

CHAPTER 3

SULPHIDES, PAPERWEIGHTS, AND PORTRAIT BUSTS

THE use of 'sulphides' or 'cameo incrustations', a novelty that appeared in England earlier in the century, continued into the Victorian period. Although the art was attempted by a Bohemian manufacturer as early as 1750 and somewhat later by French manufacturers, the introduction of sulphides in England was the work of Apsley Pellatt the younger at the Falcon Glassworks, London, who first patented his methods in 1819. The sulphides were small white paste figures, usually portrait medallions, coats of arms, masks, or, less frequently, flowers or small landscapes, which were embedded in clear crystal glass. The first publication of Pellatt's method came in his *Memoir on the Origin, Progress and Improvement of Glass Manufactures, including an account of the Patent Crystallo Ceramie, or Glass Incrustations*, published in London in 1821. The process was later described in more detail in his *Curiosities of Glass Making* (London, 1849). The sulphides themselves were made of china clay and super-silicate of potash (that is, sand, with a small portion of carbonate of potash, heated in a crucible) ground and mixed in such proportions that it could be cast in a plaster-of-Paris mould. The sulphides or cameos were then baked and cooled, being reheated before they were incorporated into the hot, molten glass. Pellatt applied this method of decoration to a wide variety of glass articles – decanters and wine glasses, tumblers, mugs, plates, lamps, girandoles, lustres, chimney ornaments and door plates – and to smaller articles such as scent bottles, doorknobs and paperweights, and for mounting as brooches, ear-rings and other items of jewellery. The 1821 volume illustrates designs for most of these articles. The cameos have a white silvery appearance when set in the glass and where appropriate the object itself was embellished with high-quality diamond and strawberry cutting. A number of the pieces are signed by Pellatt or have the words 'Patent London'. Pellatt also stated that the cameo incrustations could be enamelled or painted with metallic colours and illustrated a toilet bottle and a water jug decorated with a coloured rose. Although a number of Baccarat pieces with enamelled sulphides exist, there appear to be no extant Pellatt pieces, although the Pellatt jewel-mounted cameos that survive are set against coloured backgrounds, giving the effect of a Wedgwood Jasper cameo.

Although most of Pellatt's sulphides seem to have been made soon after the issue of his first patent, the production of them at the Falcon Glassworks continued well into the Victorian period, and examples were included in the firm's display at the Great Exhibition of 1851. Among Pellatt's Victorian sulphide examples were paperweights with the head of Prince Albert and several with views of the Crystal Palace and a perfume bottle with the head of Queen Victoria, which are now in the collections of the Glenbow-Alberta Institute in Calgary, Canada. Other firms produced sulphides for paperweights during the Victorian period. Two different versions showing the Crystal Place are signed by Allen & Moore of Great Hampton Row, Birmingham.

This firm, a partnership formed by Joseph Moore (1817–1892), the medallist and die sinker, and John Allen, also a die sinker and

Two paperweights (above) and two door knobs (p. 43) with sulphides made by John Ford, Holyrood Glass Works, Edinburgh, *c.* 1880. 19 George Heriot, signed '. . . WOOD' (?) h. 2¾ in. 20 Robert Burns, signed 'MOORE' for Joseph Moore, 1817–92, h. 2⅛ in.

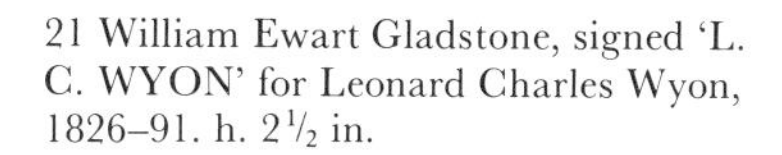

21 William Ewart Gladstone, signed 'L. C. WYON' for Leonard Charles Wyon, 1826–91. h. $2^1/_2$ in.

22 Queen Anne. diam $2^1/_4$ in. *Royal Scottish Museum, Edinburgh.*

inventor, lasted from 1844 to 1856. Apart from paperweights, Allen and Moore also produced articles of papier mâché, metal vases, cups and boxes, and they exhibited in the general hardware section at the Great Exhibition of 1851. The Allen & Moore paperweights are both circular. One has a view of the building in the top half surmounted by the words 'The building at London for the International Exhibition 1851' and the lower half has tiny profile protraits of the Queen and Prince Albert, flanked by putti, and the inscriptions 'J. Paxton Esq., Architect' and 'Allen & Moore'. The other version has a similar view of the building with the words 'The Building for the International Exhibition' round the top and 'London 1851' below the building with the initials 'A & M'. Two other signed Allen & Moore weights are known, one with a profile of the Duke of Wellington, the other with a circular sulphide medallion of Edward VII as a boy, dressed in sailor costume, with the inscription 'Britain's Hope, The Prince of Wales'.

Pellatt's process was a complicated and expensive operation and with the advent of pressed glass various firms seem to have experimented with imitating true sulphides by filling press-moulded indentations with plaster, which looked fairly convincing from the front. None of these experiments were really successful as the decoration could only be applied cold. Later in the century, however, from about 1880, the firm of John Ford, Holyrood Glassworks, Edinburgh, made considerable use of Pellatt's process. Like Pellatt, Ford produced a wide range of glass objects decorated with sulphides, including spirit bottles and decanters, vases, lamps, doorknobs and paperweights. The sulphides were usually medallion heads of notables, including Prince Albert and earlier royalties such as Queen Anne; politicians such as Wellington and Gladstone; poets such as Shakespeare and Byron, but with a special emphasis on Scottish heroes, notably Robert Burns and Sir Walter Scott; and George Heriot, the famous Edinburgh goldsmith who was jeweller to James VI of Scotland (James I of England). The cameo heads of the Holyrood Glassworks were generally of high quality and were often by, or after, leading medallists. They include a fine head of Gladstone signed 'L. C. Wyon F', an example of which is in the Royal Scottish Museum at Edinburgh (Plate 21). Leonard Charles Wyon (1826–91), the son of William Wyon, was an engraver at the Royal Mint. The same Wyon head of Gladstone appears on a finely cut Ford vase in the collection of Paul Jokelson, author of an extensive volume on sulphides (Paul Jokelson, *Sulphides: The Art of Cameo Incrustation*, New York, 1968). The Royal Scottish Museum also has a Burns paperweight signed 'Moore' – for Joseph Moore – and probably produced after he set up on his own with his son and other assistants (following the dissolution of his partnership with Allen) first at Summer Lane and later at Pitsford Street, Birmingham.

John Ford & Company used sulphide decorations on a whole series of spirit decanters and toilet water or scent bottles. Most of the spirit decanters are tall and narrow, decorated with brilliant cutting, with lapidary stoppers, and are typical of the current shapes of the 1880s (Plate 24). Although the sulphide heads were uniform, being confined mostly to Shakespeare, Byron, and above all Burns, the surrounding decoration showed considerable variety. Some were intaglio engraved as well as cut. For example, one Burns decanter has the sulphide head enclosed in an oval panel with 'Robert Burns' and two crossed laurel sprays engraved around it, the whole enclosed with intaglio engraving of leafy sprays with split cutting above and below, while in another the same head of Burns is set on a band engraved with scenes of Burns at the plough and the national emblem of Scotland, again with brilliant cutting. Yet another decanter with the same head, in the Glenbow-Alberta Institute, has no cutting, but finely engraved sprays of hops and barley. These decanters were made in the 1880s and, although the subjects of some of the paperweights and the toilet water bottle (the Duke of Wellington [Plate 23] and Prince Albert) would suggest an earlier date, the fact that they were presented to the Royal Scottish Museum by the firm in 1881 would indicate that all these sulphide productions were of approximately the same date.

Portraiture was represented in a more direct way by moulded glass busts. The glass was blown into moulds and was usually given a semi-matt surface by grinding or abrasion. The busts of Queen Victoria and Prince Albert, shown in Plate 26, are marked 'PUBLISHED BY F & C OSLER 44 OXFORD ST LONDON MAY 1ST 1845'. Copies of these busts by F. & C. Osler, whose glass-works were in Broad Street, Birmingham, were shown at the Great Exhibition of 1851, together with similar busts of Shakespeare, Milton, Sir Walter Scott and Robert Peel. Osler's also produced a glass statuette called 'A Sleeping Child'.

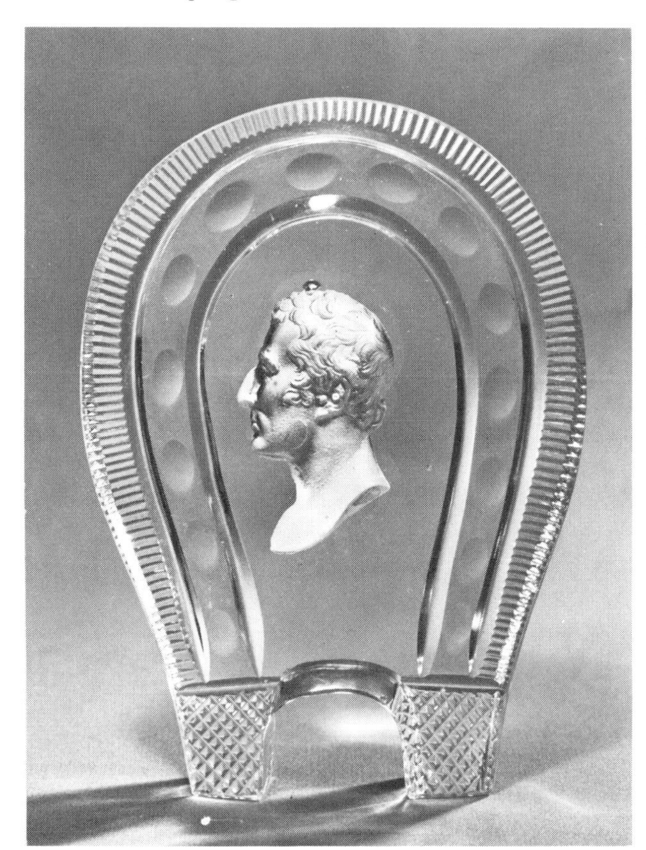

23 Paperweight with cameo head of Duke of Wellington. Diamond-engraved 'Wellington' and 'Holyrood Glass Works'. Made by John Ford. *c.* 1880. h. 5 in. *Royal Scottish Museum, Edinburgh.*

24 Scent bottle with cameo head of the Prince Consort. Made by John Ford, Holyrood Glass Works. *c.* 1880. h. 7$^1/_4$ in. *Royal Scottish Museum, Edinburgh.*

Another Birmingham firm, Lloyd & Summerfield, produced similar busts of the Queen and Prince Albert, which they showed at the 1851 Exhibition, together with glass medallion busts of the Duke of Wellington and Sir Robert Peel in glass frames.

Later, in the 1870s, similar portrait busts were made by John Ford of Edinburgh, including busts of Pope Pius IX, and Disraeli, and also a statuette of the Virgin. Akin to these portrait figures were the pair of comports or candlesticks made by John Ford with a figure of a boy gardener with a basket on his head, with a milkmaid with a pail as his companion, both figures being in eighteenth-century dress (Plate 27). The basket and the pail supported shallow bowls engraved with ferns, to form comports, or could be used simply as candlesticks.

The fashion for millefiori glass paperweights came from France, where they had been introduced in about 1845 and, from the onset, imported into England in considerable quantities. It was not surprising that English manufacturers should seek to copy them, but the English examples are generally less sophisticated and elaborate than

25 Scent bottle and paperweight with millefiori decoration by W. H., B. & J. Richardson, Stourbridge. *c.* 1850. *Private collection.*

those of French origin. The majority of English weights have simple millefiori decoration, that is a series of coloured glass canes embedded in the base, which are magnified by the dome of clear glass above them. The same technique was used to decorate the base of inkwells and for doorknobs. The millefiori paperweights made by George Bacchus & Sons of Birmingham were praised by the *Art Union* of 1848 'for their novelty and excellence'. Bacchus showed millefiori paperweights (which they called 'letter weights') at the Birmingham Exhibition of 1849 and in the same year the *Art Journal* noted that they were also being made by Rice Harris & Son of the Islington Glass Works, Birmingham. A number of surviving weights with some of the canes lettered 'IGW' presumably emanated from that factory. Richardson's of Stourbridge also produced similar paperweights and inkwells or bottles (Plate 25) decorated by the same means, and they were also made by James Powell & Sons and other firms. These paperweights seem to have been sold in stationers' shops rather than by the glass and china dealers. This was certainly the case with the later souvenir and pressed-glass paperweights.

26 Pair of busts of Queen Victoria and Prince Albert, moulded and finished with an abraded surface. Made by F. & C. Osler, Broad Street, Birmingham. 1845. Marked 'PUBLISHED BY F. & C. OSLER 44 OXFORD ST. LONDON. MAY 1ST. 1845'. h. $9^3/_4$ in. and $9^5/_8$ in. *Victoria & Albert Museum.*

The scenic glass paperweights, which were made in England as well as on the Continent, were made certainly as early as 1851 although most surviving examples are later. A print, often coloured by hand, was fixed to the bottom of a dome-shaped piece of glass which magnified the view. Occasionally, small pieces of tinsel were fixed behind the windows of a building to enhance the effect. A number were produced showing views of the Crystal Palace Great Exhibition Building of 1851. One, showing the exterior was registered by Berens, Blumberg & Co. of St Paul's Churchyard, London, in October 1851. Since Berens, Blumberg & Co. were wholesalers rather than manufacturers, and importers of foreign glass, this weight may be of continental origin. The same is true of six paperweights showing an exterior view and five of the internal courts of the Crystal Palace when it was moved to Sydenham in 1854. These were registered by George Novra of 45A Regent Street, London in July and August 1854.

John Ford & Company, Holyrood Glass Works, Edinburgh, produced a series of oval scenic paperweights with Edinburgh views.

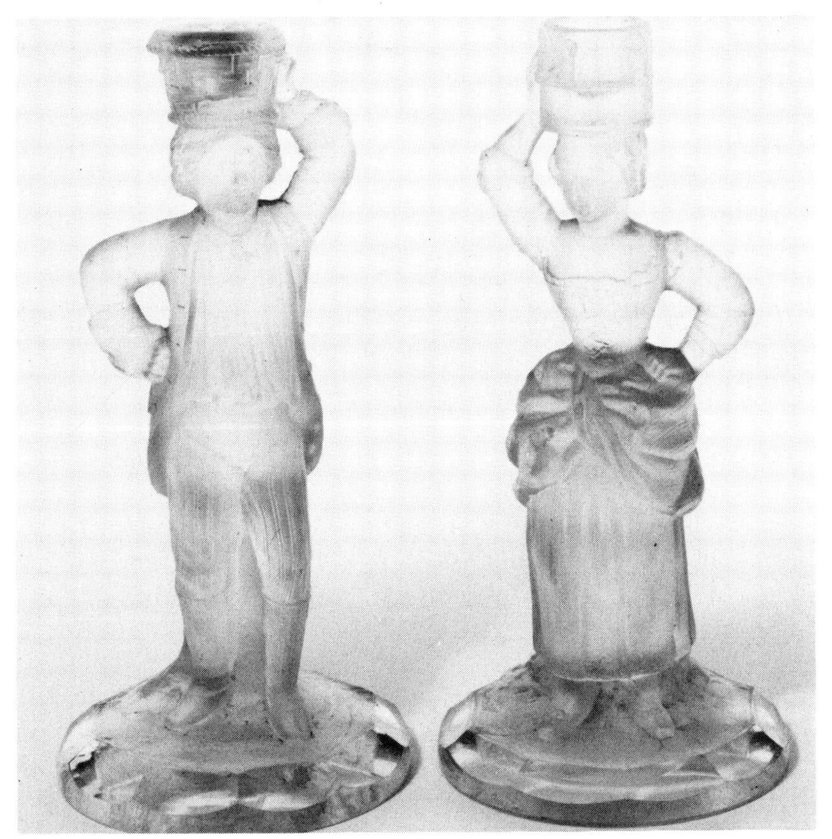

27 Pair of figures in clear colourless moulded glass with abraded surface, used as candlesticks or bases for shallow glass dishes forming comports or tazzas. Made by John Ford, Holyrood Glass Works, Edinburgh. *c.* 1870–5. h. 9¾ in. *Sotheby's Belgravia.*

One of these with a view of the Burns Monument and Arthur's Seat is illustrated in a catalogue of about 1868 with a caption, 'Letter-weights, Edinburgh Views – 9s., 13s.6d., 17s.6d., 22s.6d. a dozen' – presumably according to size or whether the prints were plain or coloured.

Whereas the early scenic paperweights were mostly dome-shaped, after about 1870 ovals, oblongs, hearts and other fancy shapes became increasingly common. In later examples photographs were often used rather than prints. The later weights were also used extensively for advertising purposes as well as for souvenirs of seaside resorts and other tourist attractions. Some of these weights incorporate pressed fancy borders surrounding the picture.

A circular weight with a press-moulded portrait bust of Queen Victoria, surrounded by a series of raised beads, was probably made by Sowerby's Ellison Glass Works, as it is very similar in style to their 1887 Jubilee Plate. The impressed design was intended to be gilded but in most extant examples this gilding has worn away. A similar paperweight, with an impressed design of the Prince of Wales feathers, is illustrated in a Sowerby & Company catalogue of 1894. An earlier catalogue of 1892 shows a paperweight of a cat on a shoe, made in both clear and roughened glass. This, like the other paperweights discussed in the chapter on Pressed Glass, were more often sold in pairs and were intended to be used as mantelpiece ornaments rather than as paperweights.

In the latter part of the nineteenth century rough green bottle glass paperweights were made in a tall beehive shape, the larger ones being intended for use as door-stops. These weights are often known as 'dumps' and usually contain the representation of a flower, or group of flowers, or an arrangement of spaced air bubbles, the flowers or bubbles having an almost metallic, silvery appearance. Some surviving examples have the same stamp on the base as the bottles made by Kilner Brothers of Thornhill Lees and Conisboro', and other Yorkshire bottle-makers, including one at Knottingly, appear to have made similar examples. One weight made at Knottingly, now in the Tolson Memorial Museum at Huddersfield, encloses a ceramic bust of Queen Victoria, commemorating her 1887 Jubilee.

CHAPTER 4

PAINTED AND ENAMELLED GLASS

ONE OF the leading producers of painted and printed glass in the 1840s was the Stourbridge firm of W. H., B. & J. Richardson, who made both opaline and clear glass decorated by painting, printing and gilding. Fortunately, most of the Richardson glass of this period can be identified by inscriptions painted or printed on the base, by registration marks, or by comparison with the drawings in an extant pattern book in the possession of Brierley Hill Public Library. The most common Richardson marks are the words 'RICHARDSON'S STOURBRIDGE' inscribed in a circle enclosing the pattern number, or 'RICHARDSON'S' on a ribbon scroll with the word 'VITRIFIED' below. Some pieces have only the pattern number, such as 'P 361', which ties up with the numbers in the pattern book mentioned above.

Many of the Richardson pieces are transfer-printed and painted with classical figure subjects, copied from Greek vase paintings, or, in one instance, from the Portland Vase. The figure subjects are combined with Greek ornament, including variants of the Greek key pattern, and various anthemion motifs, picked out in gilding. The vessels include vases, jugs and matching goblets (Plate 30). The jugs are especially characteristic, with low, rounded bellies and a three-lipped mouth deriving from the British revival of interest in Greek pottery in the 1840s, the shape itself harmonising admirably with the decoration. Most of the vases are also classical in inspiration, sometimes in the form of a two-handled urn or amphora. Opaline glass, left either smooth or roughened by abrasion to give a matt surface, was the most common vehicle for this type of decoration. The pair of enamelled vases illustrated in Plate 28, although of clear glass, are said to have been made by Richardson's. The classical figures are painted in terracotta and gilt in a style that would at the time have been termed 'Etruscan'.

Similar opalescent glass decorated with figures in 'Etruscan' style was made by Thomas Webb and reviewed in the *Art Union* for 1847 (p. 222). The products included vases, jugs, bowls and goblets, some painted simply in red and black, others painted in a full range of colours. According to the *Art Union*, the vessels were painted in the workshops of Thomas Battam & Son, Gough Square, to the order of Mr Gilles, of Bartlett's Buildings, Holborn, then the centre of the London glass showrooms. Battam & Son also painted similar 'Etruscan' figure designs on ceramics. Most of the designs were copied from the vases in the collection of Sir William Hamilton or from the designs of Flaxman, but they, like Richardson's, also drew inspiration from the Portland Vase.

The firm of George Bacchus & Sons, Birmingham, also produced opaline vases with printed decoration of classical figures derived from Greek vases (Plate 29), and Davis, Greathead and Green of Stourbridge showed painted glass imitations of Greek pottery at the 1851 Exhibition which are illustrated in the official descriptive catalogue.

Another firm which not only drew inspiration from the shape and decoration of Greek pottery but sought to imitate the ware itself, was the London firm of J. F. Christy of Lambeth. The vase shown on Plate 31 is of black glass painted in red and black in a close imitation of a Greek red figure vase.

Other jugs and goblets by Richardson's were decorated not with classical subjects, but with Near Eastern or Biblical subjects, with Arabs and palm trees, water-carriers and the like, executed in monochrome sepia.

Another range of Richardson's painted glass was decorated with water-lilies. The clear glass jug shown in Plate 32 is marked on the base 'Richardson's Vitrified' and bears a diamond registration mark indicating that it was registered on 13 June 1848. Several variants of this water-lily design occur in the Richardson pattern books. Similar jugs and goblets of opaque glass, also decorated with water-lilies, were shown by Rice Harris & Son, of the Islington Glass Works, Birmingham, at the Dublin Exhibition of 1853.

Some of the Richardson jugs decorated with water-lilies have twisted rope handles, with twisted stems to the matching goblets. The water-lily designs were also used for etched and gilded decoration. Matching carafes and cups, finger bowls and lipped wine-glass coolers were also made. A similar range was produced with enamelled bulrushes on both plain and opaline glass. Jugs and goblets of the same shapes, also dating from the period 1845 to 1850, were painted with irises or seaweed, the decoration springing from the base of the jug or the bowl of the goblet. It is possible that some of this decoration was executed by George Hancock, a ceramic artist who worked for the Derby factory and elsewhere for many years before joining Richardson's towards the end of his life. A surviving pattern of this type of decoration, in the Richardson archives, is inscribed 'G. Hancock'.

Other Richardson pieces, especially vases, are painted with free floral designs, accurately depicted in their natural colours, in a manner that has a distinct affinity with the French opalines of the same period (Plate 33). Local tradition maintains that some of the more elaborate floral pieces (Plate 34) were painted by Thomas Bott

28 Clear glass vases painted in red enamel and gilt in the 'Etruscan' style. Said to be made by W. H., B. & J. Richardson, Stourbridge. *c.* 1848. h. $10^1/_4$ in. *Victoria & Albert Museum.*

(b. 1829) who joined Kerr & Binns at Worcester in 1852, becoming famous for his white enamel painting on Worcester 'Limoges' ware. The French influence on Richardson's glass is also seen in jugs and vases that are decorated with scrolls and formal leaf and flower ornament in gilt. One pattern for painted decoration in the French style is inscribed 'painted by Lawrence', but so far this artist has not been identified.

The French influence seen in these Richardson pieces, can also be observed in a vase by J. F. Christy of Lambeth, now in the Victoria & Albert Museum, which is painted with a pair of lovers in mid-eighteenth-century French costume. While the painting on these English pieces is usually less elaborate than on contemporary French examples, it is usually more sophisticated and better executed than that on many Bohemian examples of the same period.

Richardson also produced spirit bottles, in yellow and in white opaline glass, decorated with printed decoration. The decoration consisted of the name of the spirit that the bottle was to contain – GIN, WHISKY or RUM – each letter being composed of a human figure contorted into the shape of the letter, the whole being enclosed in a wreath of wine or hops.

Some interesting pieces of enamelled glass were made expressly for Felix Summerly's Art Manufactures, the enterprise started by Sir Henry Cole (1808–82) in 1847. Sir Henry Cole, author, member of the Executive Committee for the Great Exhibition of 1851 and Secretary of the Department of Science and Art at South Kensington from 1855–77, was prominent as a design theoretician. In 1845 he won a Society of Arts prize for a tea-set he had designed (under the pseudonym of Felix Summerly). Encouraged by this success, he decided that if prominent painters and sculptors could be persuaded to design articles of everyday use, it might do much to improve public taste and raise the standard of manufactures. Accordingly, in 1847, he founded Felix Summerly's Art Manufactures, an enterprise that lasted for about three years, until pressure of work on the forthcoming Great Exhibition led Cole to abandon the project. One of the leading artists that Cole commissioned was Richard Redgrave, who designed the 'Well Spring' – a water jug, carafe or vase with a design of water plants enamelled in their natural colours, made by John Fell Christy of Stangate Glass Works, Lambeth, and registered on 3 June 1847. The water jug version is illustrated in

29 Opaque white glass vase with transfer-printed and painted decoration in the 'Etruscan' style made by George Bacchus & Sons, Birmingham. Marked 'GEO. BACCHUS & SONS VITRIFIED ENAMEL COLOURS'. 1845–50. h. $13^{5}/_{8}$ in. *Victoria & Albert Museum*.

Plate 35; the jug had one gilt handle and the vase two gilt handles. A small-scale version of the vase was also made in porcelain. According to Felix Summerly's own *Catalogue of Art Manufactures* (Chiswick, 1848) these articles were described by the *Spectator* as 'among the most beautiful designs – the materials conducive to the effect at once modestly sober and gay, cool and sparkling'. There was a matching goblet, the 'Water Lily', the bowl representing the flower, enamelled in natural colours and gilt and with a blue twisted stem, also made by Christy and registered on 25 October of the same year. It is perhaps surprising that Redgrave should have designed such decoration, as it ran quite contrary to his principles as set out in the *Manual of Design*, the official South Kensington handbook published in 1876. Writing of the special qualities of glass, Redgrave stated that 'the perfect transparency is another rare quality, whereby the purity and the clearness of the liquid it may serve to contain is immediately manifest enabling the satisfied eye to minister directly to the pleasures of taste'. Elaborating this point, he stressed that the foremost qualities:

'are its brilliancy of surface and transparency, both of which

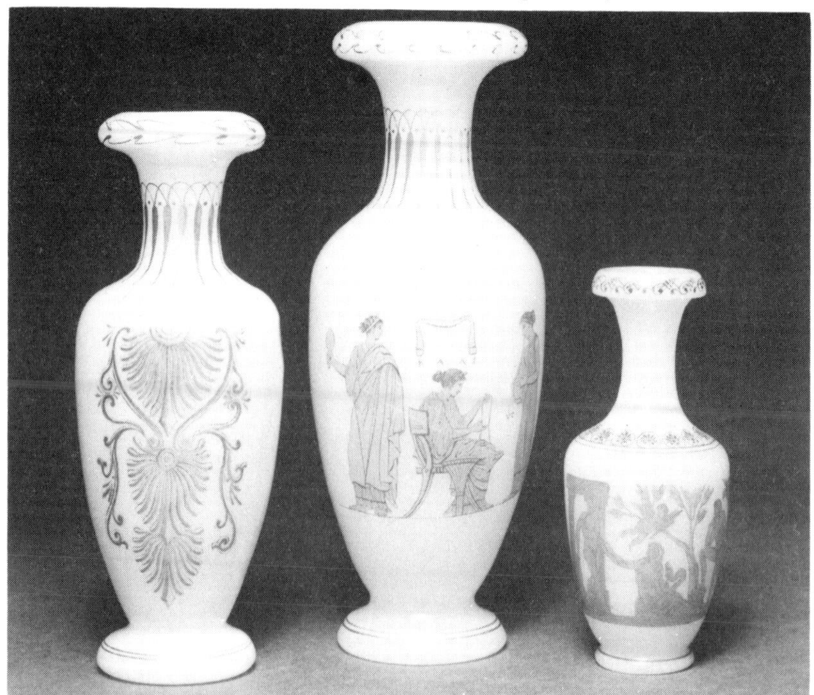

30 Three opaline vases with printed and gilt decoration in the 'Etruscan' style made by W. H., B. & J. Richardson, Stourbridge. Marked 'RICHARDSON'S VITRIFIED' and with pattern numbers. The smallest vase has a design taken from the Portland Vase. 1848–50. h. 8½ in., 9¾ in. and 6 in. *Private collection.*

31 Vase of dark blue (nearly black) glass with painted decoration in pinkish enamel in the 'Etruscan' style. Made by John Fell Christy, Stangate Glass Works, Lambeth. Marked 'Stangate, London'. *c.* 1849. h. $12^7/_8$ in. *Victoria & Albert Museum.*

> should be preserved with the greatest care in all right treatments of glass. And yet, strange to say, these qualities are not only often disregarded but there is a strong tendency to destroy them: thus we see wine glasses and decanters, water bottles, caraffes (sic) and drinking vessels of many kinds, not only with the surface covered with ground ornament, but sometimes wholly and entirely changed and obscured by grinding so as to render them perfectly opaque: or, we have colour most ingeniously applied to destroy purity and prevent a proper enjoyment of the glowing lustre of the liquid contents; whilst sometimes the material is wholly or partially opalised.'

He then explains that the beautiful shapes that can be achieved by blowing should only be decorated by narrow bands of engraved ornament and that 'this ornament ought to be reserved for those parts of the bowl which do not interfere with the sight of the contents . . . any gilding or enamelling can only be admirable under the above rule'. As we have seen, virtually the whole contents of Redgrave's 'Well Spring' carafe and 'Water Lily' goblet would have been obscured by his heavy enamelled decoration. Redgrave also designed a 'Tendril' wine glass and 'Vine' finger bowl for Felix Summerly, both made by Richardson's, and illustrated in the *Journal of Design* (vol. I, 1849, p. 17). The wine glass had vine leaves enamelled in gold on the bowl and a thread of green glass was wound spirally round the stem, giving the glass its name. On the finger bowl – a footed bowl with a flaring, crimped top – the wine leaves were enamelled in natural colours, with a band of tendrils in gilt above, The *Journal of Design* remarked that these items must necessarily be costly in manufacture 'as, indeed, must all ornamental [art] which demands skilled hand labour'. However, Redgrave also designed some simpler items for Felix Summerly; the 'Flask' decanters with gilt enamel or parian stoppers, with wine glasses to match, which could be had plain or gilded, but even these were relatively expensive – the gilded carafes retailing at three guineas each and the wine glasses at six shillings.

Other glass produced for Felix Summerly Art Manufactures by Richardson's were a champagne and soda water glass called 'Bubbles Bursting' designed by H. J. Townsend. As with the other Summerly products, the ornament was considered appropriate to the function of the object. The design consisted of a naked boy, surrounded by vine tendrils and grapes, holding a wine skin. Jets of wine, as from a fountain, burst up from the skin and in the jets eight naked babies disported themselves. The design could be either painted or printed in gold on the glass, or engraved, the price varying accordingly. In the same illustrative manner was a glass bread or cake dish, designed by John Absolon, ornamented with the Sower, the Reaper, the Gleaner and the Miller in gilt enamelling. Similarly, a set of ivory and wood salad servers, called the 'Endive', modelled by the sculptor John Bell, was accompanied by a ruby glass salad bowl which was described as being 'in keeping'.

Apart from these objects, which are described and sometimes

32 Clear glass jug painted in natural colours, made by Richardson's of Stourbridge. Marked 'RICHARDSON'S VITRIFIED' and with diamond registry mark. 1848. h. 9¾ in. *Victoria & Albert Museum.*

illustrated in the various catalogues of the Summerly Art Manufactures, the Victoria & Albert Museum possesses a number of other designs for glass for this enterprise which may or may not have been carried out. One is of a simple finger glass in a waved pattern which anticipates the range of glasses designed by Philip Webb in 1860. This design is by John Bell as are designs for a wine glass and tumbler with applied circular prunts and a snake and claw flower tazza to be made 'in white opal or frosted glass with the scales of the snake touched with gold'. The snake coiled round the stem of the tazza is very similar to those produced by Richardson's. The tazza, or bowl, was supplied with a clip-on domed cover of gilded wire mesh anticipating the popular rose bowls of the Edwardian era and later. Henry Cole himself designed a spiral glass candlestick to be made by Apsley Pellatt & Company but no actual example or illustration of this appears to have survived. Indeed, it is quite

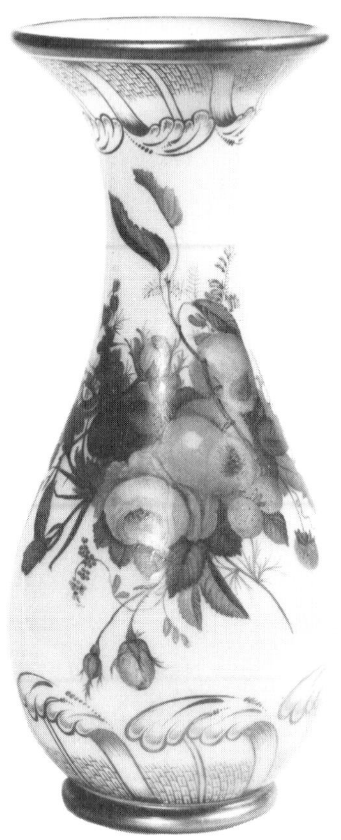

33 White opaline vase, painted in natural colours and gilt, possibly by Thomas Bott. Made by Richardson's of Stourbridge. *c.* 1850. h. 12 in. *Borough of Stourbridge Collection.*

possible that a number of the listed items were never made, or, if they were, only in limited quantities, as, apart from the comparatively few specimens in public collections, they are rarely seen. Since the catalogue states that 'the Copyrights of all the Art Manufactures are protected either by the Registration Acts or by the several Copyright Acts', and most suriviving specimens bear the diamond registration mark, the monogram 'F.S.' and other initials or names of manufacturers and designers, identification should be relatively simple.

Gold enamelling seems to have been a speciality of the Summerly Art Manufactures and, earlier in the century in the mid-1830s, and slightly later, Thomas Hawkes of Dudley featured 'gold enamel' wares and produced some spectacular pieces that combined a number of techniques including printing or etching, painting and gilding. A set of gold enamel plates was made for the first reception given to Queen Victoria by the Corporation of London after her

34 Pair of opaline vases painted with convolvulus and fuchsia in natural colours and gilt. Made by W. H., B. & J. Richardson, Stourbridge. Marked 'RICHARDSON'S VITRIFIED'. *c.* 1850. h. 13³/₄ in. *Sotheby's Belgravia.*

Coronation in 1837. A plate in the Victoria & Albert Museum (Plate 37) is almost certainly from this service. The plate, decorated with printing, painting and gilding behind an outer layer of clear glass, has the Royal Coat of Arms in the centre, surrounded by a wreath of roses, thistles and shamrock, the whole enclosed in a kind of garter star set against a red enamelled background. An even more spectacular example, possibly made by Thomas Hawkes in the late 1830s, is the urn-shaped covered vase shown in Plate 36, also in the Victoria & Albert Museum. It is of clear crystal glass, with an ormolu knob on the cover, and a fixed glass liner to the body and cover. The inner layer is decorated by gilding, enamelling and cutting, and the outer surface is further decorated by cutting. Several other pieces with decoration by the same method, and in similar style are known, and it seems likely that they all emanated from the same glass-works. Unfortunately, none of these pieces are signed, and they have at times been described as French, but an English origin seems more likely.

35 The 'Well Spring' jug designed by Richard Redgrave for Henry Cole's 'Summerly's Art Manufactures'. Clear glass, painted in enamel colours with gilt rim. Made by J. F. Christy, Lambeth, and marked with diamond registration mark and the firm's initials in monogram. 1847. h. 10¾ in. *Sotheby's Belgravia.*

Another elaborate method of decorating glass was known as 'gem enamelling'. The *Art Journal* of 1856 illustrates some vases decorated by this process which was patented by Jennens and Betteridge, the Birmingham manufacturers of papier mâché. A pair of glass vases, about seventeen inches high, were executed for Prince Albert to the designs of Lewis Gruner. The vases were of rich purple glass, decorated with floral festoons of gold and diamonds dividing the ground into four compartments. In one compartment was a laurel wreath of emeralds with ruby scrolls surrounding the initials V and A, and in the others were the rose, thistle and shamrock executed in jewels of the appropriate colours. The base was set in electro-gilt pierced mountings by Messrs Elkington. Two other similarly decorated vases were illustrated, one with snake handles. As these vases were designed at the time Lewis Gruner was superintending the decorations of the new State Rooms at Buckingham Palace, it seems likely that the glass itself was made by F. & C. Osler of Birmingham, who supplied the chandeliers and lustres. Although the *Art Journal* commented that the 'novel and very beautiful branch of art manufacture' would doubtless be much 'inquired after', it is unlikely that, on account of the expense, much of this gem enamelled glass would have been made. However, in the late 1850s and 1860s there was a good deal of less elaborate 'jewelled' glass, enriched, not with real gem stones, but with blobs of coloured glass or enamel, and gilding. A typical example was a service shown by Apsley Pellatt & Company at the London International Exhibition of 1862. The elaborate Moorish style decoration is carried out by engraving and gilding and is enriched with beads of glass imitating rubies and emeralds. Simpler jewelled table services and vases were made by James Powell & Sons of Whitefriars and by other manufacturers.

A strange fashion in enamelled glass, dating from the 1880s, may best be described as 'zoomorphic'. The main protagonists in this field seem to have been Thomas Webb although similar items were produced by other Stourbridge firms, notably Stevens & Williams.

Reviewing Thomas Webb's exhibit at the Australian Centennial Exhibition, the *Pottery Gazette* (1 December 1888) mentions that 'a collection of vases painted in enamels includes some extraordinary shapes. Flying fish, dragons and frogs are separately moulded and fixed upon the vessel, and one vase is so elaborate that at least thirty-eight different pieces can be counted.'

36 Cased vase and cover of crystal glass, the inner layer decorated by gilding, enamelling and cutting, the outer surface further decorated by cutting. Possibly made by Thomas Hawkes of Dudley. *c.*1835–40. *Victoria & Albert Museum*.

37 Gold enamel plate decorated with printing, painting and gilding behind an outer layer of clear glass. Probably made by Thomas Hawkes of Dudley as part of a service used at the first reception for Queen Victoria by the Corporation of London after her coronation in 1837. *Victoria & Albert Museum.*

The enamelling was carried out in a workshop set up at Thomas Webb's by a French artist, Jules Barbe, in about 1880. A large bound volume showing many of the designs produced in this workshop is preserved among the archives at Thomas Webb's. It is inscribed 'Burmese, Gold Fish, Birds, etc.', and the Stationer's label inside is dated: 9.6.79. The book covers the period from 1880 to 1888, the first grotesque jug being registered in July 1879. It contains numerous designs for these strange zoomorphic pieces together with examples of more conventional enamelled and gilt ornament as well as designs for the Queen's Burmese Ware. The first designs in the book are for wine glasses with enamelled and gilt monograms. These designs are followed by a claret jug with the Prince of Wales feathers, butterflies and wild flowers in enamel and gilt (no. 195). The next design (no. 196) is also comparatively restrained, a straight-sided jug with gold fish and water in enamel colours which is marked as having been engraved first by Kny. The next hundred or so drawings are all variations on the zoomorphic theme, ranging from vessels in the forms of grotesque beasts and birds (including a cock and a duck) to jugs, goblets and vases with applied fish and handles in the form of lizards, salamanders and dragons. The animal and bird jugs are often decorated with extremely incongruous ornament. For example, one grotesque animal jug is patterned all over with daisies, while a grotesque bird has enamelled decoration in a chinoiserie style. Some of the designs are reasonably consistent in their decoration, all of the elements being associated with marine or pond life – applied fish and shells, gilt seaweed and 'coralene' decoration. Others, such as the jug illustrated in Plate 38, with its lizard handle and Japanese-style blossom and birds present a strange mixture of elements. Another lizard handle jug of the same shape is decorated with lilies-of-the-valley. One of the most bizarre is a jug with a lizard handle, and a matching goblet with a lizard stem, the bodies being covered with enamelled and gilt flowers, parrots and butterflies. In other instances the vases have applied fish feet, and insects, including bees, are used a decoration.

Although Jules Barbe's workshop was closely associated with Thomas Webb's, Barbe also seems to have executed work for other Stourbridge firms. In 1901 and 1902 the Richardson pattern books contain a number of gilded vases and centre pieces with floral decoration. The first series, marked with Barbe's pattern numbers from 185 to 194, dated October 1901, were small-scale floral patterns – sprays of daisies and leaves, convolvulus, festoons of flowers, etc. – which were executed in bright and dull gold, mostly on pea green and opal threaded bodies. The second range, dating from March 1902, had an engraved and gilt pattern of fish and pond weeds, which was marked 'Barbe's no. 192'. The third range, produced later that year, with pattern numbers from 297 to 306, was of tulips, daisies, and jasmine sprays, executed in typical art nouveau style.

The zoomorphic jugs made by Stevens & Williams do not appear to have been enamelled but were decorated with intaglio engraving. They were apparently the speciality of Tom Cartwright, who also made the blanks for the most important cameo pieces, and were made for mounting in silver by Hukin & Heath of Birmingham, the mounts being in the shape of the appropriate bird's head.

At Stevens & Williams in the 1880s and 1890s the enamelling

38 Jug with painted enamel decoration and gilding and applied furnace-wrought decoration. Made by Thomas Webb & Sons, Stourbridge, and decorated in the workshop of Jules Barbe. *c.* 1888. *Brierley Hill Collection.*

39 Jug with engraved silver deposit made by Stevens & Williams, Brierley Hill, and designed by Erard. 1886. In the possession of the makers. h. $5^3/_4$ in. *Photograph Victoria & Albert Museum.*

was done under the direction of Oscar Pierre Erard, who, like Jules Barbe, was a Frenchman. A low comport made by Stevens & Williams enamelled with a floral design in the Persian style, probably by Erard himself, is now in the Northwood Collection (no. 388) at the Stourbridge Council House. The Persian style was also favoured by Thomas Webb. A particularly elaborate service of some 300 pieces, decorated in the Persian style in two shades of raised gold, occupied the principal decorators of the Barbe workshop for nearly a year and was completed in July 1888, being destined for the American market.

Erard was also responsible for decorating glass with a silver deposit which was then engraved (Plate 39). Most of the silver deposit pieces were in Persian, Indian or other Oriental styles. Another innovation at Stevens & Williams was their 'Tapestry' glass, registered in 1887. The closely trailed surface of the glass, combined with the painted decoration, gave the effect of the horizontal ribs of a woven tapestry. Once again, most of the decoration of the 'tapestry' glass, carried out by Erard, was in Persian, Indian or other Oriental styles.

CHAPTER 5

NAILSEA GLASS AND FRIGGERS

THE so-called 'Nailsea' glass, which is associated more with the late eighteenth and early nineteenth centuries, continued to be made during the Victorian period. The Nailsea glass-works were set up near Bristol in 1788 by John Robert Lucas and survived under successive partnerships until 1873. Although this factory has given its name to a vast range of 'peasant' or popular glass, only a small proportion of extant examples is likely to have actually emanated from Nailsea, or nearby Bristol, as it was made in most glass-making centres, both in England and in Scotland.

The range of 'Nailsea' glass is extensive, comprising domestic articles such as jugs, sugar basins and milk jugs; gimmels, bellows, pocket and other flasks; novelties and friggers including rolling pins, walking sticks, pipes, horns and other trifles. Much of this glass, particularly the domestic ware, was made of bottle glass and was an off-shoot of the bottle-making industry. It was also an attempt to evade the heavy excise duty on flint glass by making domestic items in good-quality bottle glass, which was taxed at a much lower rate. The shapes generally bear little relation to those of the more fashionable and sophisticated lead crystal glass and have more affinity with simple pottery shapes than those of the contemporary glassware. The jugs are often pitcher-shaped but rather freely blown with applied handles and are found in various shades of green, some with an amber or brownish tone, and are decorated in a variety of ways. Some have encircling bands of white enamel on the body, others have combed festoon stripes, while many have a haphazard pattern of spots and splashes, usually in white, but sometimes with other

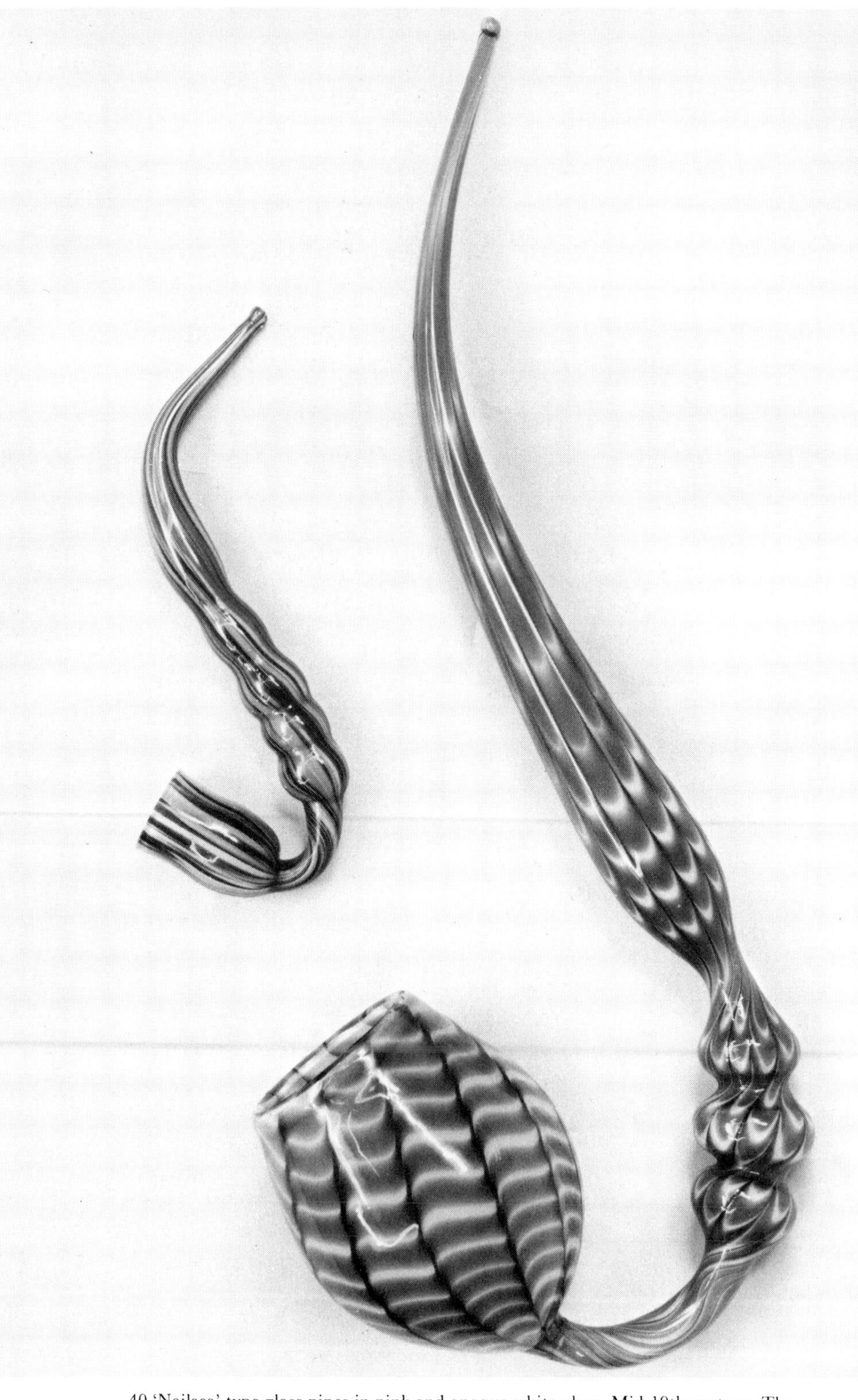

40 'Nailsea' type glass pipes in pink and opaque white glass. Mid-19th century. The larger pipe, overall l. 18 in. *Sotheby's Belgravia*.

colours. The neck of the jug often has an applied white rim. The smaller cream jugs are less frequently decorated with white enamel but may often have trailed threads round the neck. There is little documentary evidence as to exactly where this simple domestic glassware was made. One typical specimen, now in the Victoria & Albert Museum, was certainly made at a glass-house at Wrockwardine in Shropshire and other pieces, especially some in clear glass, are known to have been made in Warrington, and there is little doubt that glass-houses in the north-east, in Yorkshire, the Stourbridge area, Birmingham and Scotland, also contributed their share of 'Nailsea' glass.

After the repeal of the excise duties in 1845, which coincided with the development of cheap pressed glass, the demand for bottle glass domestic ware evidently declined but the production of novelties and friggers continued and even increased in popularity.

The glass rolling pins (Plate 41), which are traditionally supposed to have been made for sailors to give to their wives and sweethearts, were made in bottle glass, decorated with stripes and splodges, and also in deep blue and opaque white glass. The latter types were usually painted, in unfired colours and gilt, with mottoes and inscriptions, simple flower motifs and with sailing ships. The mottoes and inscriptions usually imply that the rolling pin was to be given as a present, and examples are found with the words 'For My Sister', 'Forget Me Not', 'Love the Giver' and 'To a Friend'. A number include the date and most dated examples seem to emanate from the mid-nineteenth century. Many of the rolling pins are thought to have been in the north-east and some seem to have been made at the Alloa Glass Works, including some decorated with the familiar chip-work engraving found on Alloa bottles, dated examples of which are found as late as 1878.

Most of the flasks were made in clear glass and decorated with pink and white spiral or festooned decoration or with latticinio, and often further embellished with pincered trails. The gimmel, or twin flask, was formed by two bottles, blown individually and fused together, with two spouts formed by the necks, usually pointing in opposite directions. Others were made in the form of hand bellows, again in clear glass with similar decoration. These, as well as simple single flasks, were made to contain toilet water and perfume, or perhaps oil and vinegar, but larger glass bellows were made with a foot purely as an ornament to stand on a mantelpiece. A collection of these, dating from the 1840s and 1850s, traditionally said to have been made locally, is in the Municipal Museum and Art Gallery at Warrington, and similar examples, said to have been made at Sowerby's Ellison Glass Works can be found at the Saltwell Park Museum, Gateshead.

Glass bells (Plate 42) were another popular novelty which had a pure, resonant tone if they were made in flint glass. They were similarly decorated with enamel stripes and festoons in white and coloured glass and in ruby, purple and blue glass. They were made throughout the Victorian period and are made today and a vast number of glass bells on the market, purporting to be antique, are undoubtedly fakes of recent manufacture.

Apart from flasks and glass bells, other friggers and novelties are well represented at the Saltwell Park Museum, including pipes, walking sticks and hats, made by the workers at Sowerby's Ellison Glassworks probably in the 1870s. The walking sticks, examples of which can also be found at Warrington, were made in clear glass and in green glass in barley sugar twist form with crook handles, or with a knob at the top, or in clear glass with ruby and white twisted threads. Pipes were made in both clear glass with white and coloured striped decoration or in ruby or clear glass and ranged in size from about one foot to three feet, the latter having exaggeratedly long stems (Plate 40).

Other novelties included glass hats and boots ranging in size from miniatures to full-scale wearable objects. It is difficult to be sure which of the objects in these classes were true 'friggers', that is, objects made by the glassworkers purely for pleasure as a demonstration of their skill and imagination, and those that were made purely for commercial purposes for sale to the general public. What is certain is that many of these objects, particularly glass swords, walking sticks, large pipes, hats and bells, were made by the glassworkers to carry in their annual trade processions.

One of the best-known descriptions is that of a Glassworkers' Procession on Friday, 12 September 1823 at Newcastle upon Tyne, where each man was required to wear a coloured sash, with the initials of the glass-works where he was employed on it, to have glass feathers in his hat, glass stars suspended by chains and drops, and to carry some sort of glass ornament in his hand. The *Tyne Mercury* (16

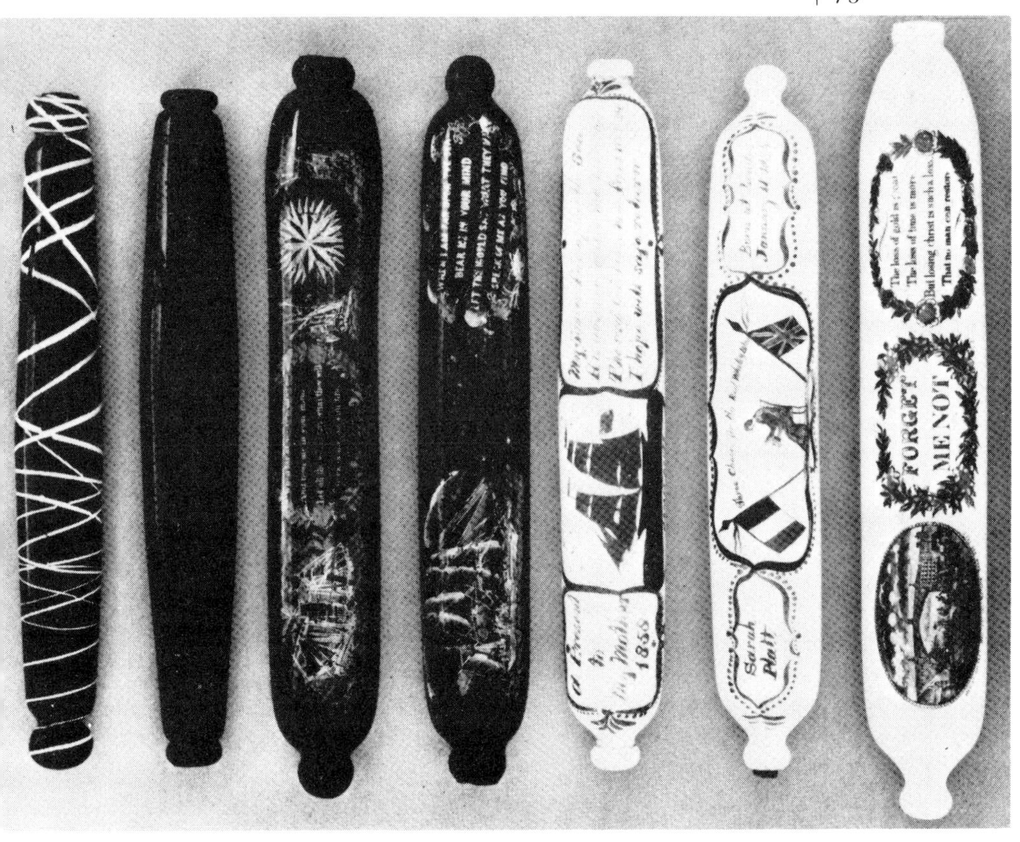

41 Group of glass rolling pins. From left to right: Dark green glass with opaque white threads. Mid-19th century. l. 15 in. Sunderland bottle glass rolling pin, finely stippled with the bridge, a railway carriage, the brig *Arun*, dated WT 1843 (details not visible on the photograph). whole l. 15 in. Amethyst glass printed with a schooner, a compass and a verse. l. 16 in. Amethyst glass printed with the *Prince of Wales* (a 74-gun ship) and a sentimental verse. l. 16 in. Opaque white glass painted with the coastal collier brig JAMES DOUSE of Shoreham, a verse, and inscription 'A Present to My Mother 1858'. l. $15^{1}/_{2}$ in. Commemorative portrait rolling pin inscribed 'Sarah Platt Born at London January 11 1834', with flags and 'Three Cheers for the Red, White and Blue'. l. $15^{1}/_{2}$ in. Opaque white glass printed with the Sunderland Bridge, 'FORGET ME NOT' and a verse, enclosed in floral wreathes. *Sotheby's Belgravia*.

42 Four glass bells in coloured and opaque clear class handles. Greatest h. 12 in. Second half of the 19th century. *Sotheby's Belgravia.*

September 1823), described the procession and listed an incredible number and variety of friggers which the glassworkers carried, alongside more conventional specimens of their art, including swords, models of glass-houses, ships, a windmill, forts with cannon, fiddles, etc.

A sword carried by John Millar of the Lemington Glassworks in the Newcastle procession of 1867 is in the Laing Art Gallery and specimens carried by John Ford's glassworkers in various Edinburgh processions are in the Huntly House Museum, Edinburgh. H. J. Haden, in his *Notes on the Stourbridge Glass Trade* (Brierley Hill, 1949), writes nostalgically of the glass-makers' annual picnic when they carried examples of their craftsmanship in procession through the streets, spectacular pieces for which the skill is now lacking. An interesting description of the contingent from the Bathgate Glass-works in the procession in support of the Franchise Bill on 4 October 1884 is given in the *West Lothian Courier* (11 October 1884):

> A large company of men at the front, led by a man on horseback. . . wore heavy helmets composed of glass, and were armed with swords and spears of the same brittle material, whilst the general body carried fancy vases, wine glasses and goblets, and different articles of every kind of coloured glass. On a large cut-glass globe, beautifully ornamented with Scotch thistles, were the words on one side: 'We will cut up the House of Lords' and on the other: 'The Franchise for the People'. Another attractive piece of work was a large etched globe ornamented most artistically showing the Franchise Bill in the process of being nibbled by a mouse, the latter representing the House of Lords, falling to the ground. There were also models of a cottage and a workbox, in splendidly executed mosaic, about 200 pieces of different coloured glass being used in making each. A complete model of a glass-cutter working at his frame was carried aloft. . . . A feature of the contingent was a number of girls, carrying a fine selection of glass goblets and behind them a number of boys wearing the famed masher hats made of glass and carrying specimens of work at the end of glass rods.

Indeed, towards the end of the century interest in these friggers increased, and many small factories, workshops and backyard cribs concentrated on producing ruby pipes and bells, walking sticks, spun-glass ships and other ornaments which had the same popular appeal as the fancy glass centrepiece or flower stands. The more elaborate ships, castles, fountains and fanciful arrangements decorated with birds with spun-glass tails, dating from the 1840s and later, were usually protected by a glass dome, in the manner of the familiar groups of wax fruit or Berlin woolwork or silk flowers arranged in a glass vase. Good examples of these can be seen in the Pilkington Glass Museum at St Helens.

CHAPTER 6

ENGRAVED GLASS

ENGRAVING was one of the most popular methods of decorating glass throughout the Victorian period. It was eminently suitable for a wide variety of styles, from delicate small-scale patterns which could be floral or purely ornamental – to elaborate naturalistic and pictorial effects.

Wheel-engraving on glass had been developed in Germany and Bohemia, particularly in Saxony, in Nuremberg and in Prague, in the late sixteenth and early seventeenth centuries, and the earliest wheel-engraved decoration in England was probably executed by immigrant workers from Central Europe.

In the early nineteenth century, when the fashion for cut glass was at its peak, wheel-engraving was generally confined to the decoration of the bowls of wine glasses, where cutting was not suitable, and for the production of commemorative pieces. Simple floral designs, 'hop and barley' and grapevine patterns were the most popular subjects. Much of the early nineteenth-century engraving was carried out on the current rummers or goblets, but the most favoured shape for engraved decoration, particularly for commemorative pieces, was the straight-sided bucket-shaped glass. These commemorative pieces appear to have been made chiefly in the Newcastle/Sunderland area. A favourite subject was the Sunderland Bridge, which, although opened in 1796, continued to be employed throughout the 1820s, 1830s and 1840s. Sailing ships and yachts were also common subjects, the name of the ship and the date often being added to the design. Sometimes a coin of the appropriate date was inserted into the knop above the stem. The world famous

No. 9.

'Rocket' locomotive, built by George & Robert Stephenson, which was victorious at the Rainhill Trials of 1829, was also a fairly common subject.

From 1820 onwards, many of these commemorative pieces appear to have emanated from the glass-works of Edward Attwood who operated at Southwick until 1865 and at the Wear Crown Glass Company, Wearmouth from 1854 to 1869. Two of the most notable engravers of these glasses were Robert Haddock, who appears in the local directories as a glass engraver from 1827 to 1853, and Robert Pyle, who was active between 1834 and 1847. Another known local engraver was Thomas Hudson, who worked in the 1830s and 1840s, and was responsible for a somewhat naively engraved goblet depict-

43 Amphora and goblet with engraved decoration designed by F. W. Moody (1824–86) and made by Apsley Pellatt & Co. 1862. Amphora h. $11^1/_2$ in. *Victoria & Albert Museum.*

44 'Neptune' jug exhibited at the Great Exhibition of 1851 by the London glass merchant J. G. Green. The blank possibly made by W. H., B. & J. Richardson of Stourbridge. h. 13¼ in. *Victoria & Albert Museum.*

ing Neptune and seahorses, which is now in the Laing Art Gallery, Newcastle upon Tyne.

It is clear that by the 1830s the scope of glass engraving had widened and individual engravers were becoming known for their work. Pigot & Company's *National Commercial Directory* for 1828–9, lists two glass engravers at Dudley, John Bourne and William Herbert. Little is known of the former, but William Herbert, the most prominent of a family of glass engravers, worked extensively for the firm of Thomas Hawkes. A fine engraved rummer, signed by William Herbert, has a representation of the London & Aylesbury stage coach of Hearm & Co., with a wreath of hops below and which, made by Hawkes about 1835, is now in a private collection. In nearby Stourbridge, the Wood family had an important glass-engraving shop, which was well established by the 1840s. A member of the family, Thomas Wood, exhibited in his own right at the Great Exhibition of 1851.

Although the names of many of the engravers are known, unfortunately their work is rarely signed. A descendant of a glass-engraving family at Brierley Hill remembers her brother-in-law (himself a glass engraver) quoting a local saying that 'you can see the man in the glass'. This saying indicated that since the workmanship

45 Two champagne glasses with engraved bowls made by George Bacchus & Sons. *c.* 1850. h $4^7/_8$ in. and 5 in. *Victoria & Albert Museum.*

46 Three wine glasses with engraved decoration made by James Powell & Sons, Whitefriars. *c.* 1865. In the possession of the makers. h. $6^1/_2$ in., $4^1/_2$ in. and $5^3/_4$ in. *Photograph Victoria & Albert Museum.*

could be readily identified, there was no need for a signature and it was not considered proper to sign one's work. It was generally only the most important pieces that were signed, such as those made for special commissions or for display at the International Exhibitions.

By the 1840s a wide variety of glass vessels were being decorated by engraving. The broad flute-cut decanters and jugs were sometimes engraved with vine ornament on alternate flutes, as in the spirit decanter shown in Plate 5, but the globular decanter and water carafes – a shape developed in the early years of Victoria's reign – offered a wider scope to the engraver. The hemispherical or saucer-shaped bowl of champagne glasses, developed in the 1840s, was also eminently suited to delicate engraving and the two wine glasses by George Bacchus & Sons of Birmingham, dating from about 1850, are typical examples (Plate 45).

By the time of the Great Exhibition of 1851, engraving featured prominently in the decoration of table glass, particularly in the displays of the London dealers. A particularly impressive piece was the Neptune Jug, exhibited by the firm of J. G. Green (later Green & Nephew), which is now in the Victoria & Albert Museum (Plate 44). The Greek-inspired 'Oenochne' shape with a high shoulder, spreading foot and three-lipped mouth, was to become increasingly popular throughout the late 1850s and 1860s. The most common shape for engraved decanters, claret jugs and vases, throughout the later 1850s, 1860s and 1870s, was ovoid, with a spreading foot, a shape that was also classical in inspiration. This shape, which looked extremely delicate when thinly blown, was most suitable for engraving, and from the 1860s onwards, for acid-etching. The characteristic blown stopper was also ovoid, or egg-shaped, often with a small bead or knob of glass at the top, sometimes also decorated with engraving to harmonise with that on the body of the vessel. The exhibit of J. G. Green showed a wide variety of engraved styles, all on classically inspired shapes, described variously as 'Etruscan' or 'Egyptian', ranging from 'Alhambresque' and 'François Premier' ornament to more naturalistic designs of water-lilies and fuschias, flowers that were much favoured in other fields of the decorative arts in the 1850s. The exhibit of Messrs Richardson of Stourbridge also included a jug and goblet engraved with water-lilies and other engraved pieces by W. J. Muckley, who was chief designer and engraver for the firm, and later became Principal of the Manchester

School of Art. The catalogue of the 1851 Exhibition shows that while heavy cut glass, and cased and enamelled glass predominated, engraved glass was already becoming fashionable. In the 1860s the classical influence continued and, apart from classical figures, delicate patterns of engraved Greek ornament (Plate 47), particularly anthemion motifs and variants of the Greek key pattern, were much favoured for table glass. The finely engraved wine glasses by James Powell & Sons (Plate 46) are characteristic of this style and parallel designs can also be found in the extant pattern books of the 1860s of such firms as John Ford, Holyrood Glass Works, Edinburgh; Richardson's of Stourbridge; and Apsley Pellatt & Company of London. Simple patterns of finely engraved vertical lines, as in the Prince of Wales service produced by Apsley Pellatt, were also common; also diaper patterns of fleurs de lys and tiny stars, as well as more elaborate Renaissance-inspired designs (Plate 43).

The 1862 London International Exhibition saw the emergence of engraved fern patterns, a style that was to remain popular for a long period and to persist throughout the 1870s and 1880s at all levels of production, some of the later fern patterns being rather crudely executed. The fashion for ferns had already been seen in other decorative arts, notably on ceramics and printed cottons in the late

47 Decanter with engraved decoration by Apsley Pellatt & Co., London. *c.* 1862. *Private collection.*

1850s and was possibly inspired by the publication in 1855 of John Moore's *Ferns of Great Britain and Ireland, Nature Printed by Henry Bradbury.*

Although other firms, including James Powell & Sons, showed engraved fern patterns at the 1862 Exhibition (Plate 103), the credit for the introduction of fern patterns into glass engraving is said to have originated with the Edinburgh workshop of J. H. B. Millar (or Müller), a Bohemian engraver who emigrated to Scotland in the late 1850s and set up a glass-engraving workshop, staffed initially with his compatriots, but later employing mostly natives of Edinburgh, who had served their six years' apprenticeship as glass engravers. According to *The Scotsman* (8 August 1866), Mr J. H. B. Millar's workshop, an unpretentious brick building in Norton Place, employed about thirty engravers, who executed a wide variety of work – 'representations of fruit, flowers, trees, men, quadrupeds, birds, lily of the valley, ferns, heather bloom and ivy' – in fact practically every subject that it was possible to engrave on glass. The more ambitious engravings included a claret jug engraved with 'The Sleep of Sorrow and the Dream of Joy' (exhibited in Paris in 1867), taken from an engraving of the statue by Monti, one of the most popular exhibits at the 1862 Exhibition. An enormous vase, three feet high, which was exhibited in 1862, depicted the Battle of Inkerman. It was bought by the Duke of Cambridge for £160, but as it was broken at the stem before delivery, the money was not paid, and although it was proposed to substitute a silver stem it does not appear to have survived. Another speciality of Mr Millar's seems to have been the engraving of portraits on glass from photographs supplied by the customer.

The description of the workshops in the *Industries of Scotland* by David Bremner (Edinburgh, 1869) shows that in three years the workshop had expanded to employ about forty men and boys. J. H. B. Millar's engraving shop seems to have worked exclusively for Messrs Millar & Company, glass dealers and potters of 2 South Street, St Andrew Street, Edinburgh, and for John Ford's Holyrood Glass Works, the firm founded in 1812 by William Ford at the North Back of Canongate, Edinburgh, under the title of the Caledonian Glass Works. Three years later the business was transferred to a new glass-works at South Back. William Ford died in 1819 and the glass-works was leased to Bailey & Company of the Midlothian Glass Works, Portobello; John Ford, William's nephew, being a partner in the enterprise. In 1835 the partnership with Bailey was dissolved and John Ford took over the premises changing the name to the Holyrood Flint Glass Works. Two years later he was appointed Flint Glass Manufacturer in Ordinary to the Queen. Two new glass-houses were added in 1841 and in 1865 (the year of John Ford's death) the firm became known as John Ford & Company. In 1898 the firm received the Royal Warrant, being appointed 'Glass Manufacturers to Her Majesty at Edinburgh' and the firm was styled the Royal Holyrood Glass Works. The glass-works closed in 1904 although the retail side of the business was carried on until 1959, when the name of John Ford & Company finally expired. A good deal of documentary material relating to the Holyrood Flint Glass Works survives in the collections of the City Museums, Edinburgh, together with a collection of glass made by the firm.

The engraved glass from the Holyrood Glass Works is of a very high standard. A particularly interesting piece is a goblet of clear glass engraved with a view of the façade of the Royal Scottish Museum (Plate 50). Inscribed on the knop is 'MADE BY W. KEEDY IN PRESENCE OF PROFESSOR GEORGE WILSON AND HIS CLASS HOLYROOD GLASS WORKS 1858'. The goblet was presented to the Museum by William Ford in 1866.

Pictorial representations of national monuments and well-known buildings figured prominently in the engraved glass emanating from the Scottish glass-works in the 1870s and 1880s, especially on large commemorative goblets, but also on claret jugs. One of the most popular subjects was the Scott Memorial in Edinburgh. A large goblet with an engraving of the memorial surrounded by a wreath of thistles has a coin of 1870 in a hollow knop in the stem. It is illustrated by Hugh Wakefield in *19th Century British Glass* (Plate 54a) and he suggests that it may have been engraved in J. H. B. Millar's workshop. Another view of the Scott Memorial occurs on an elegant claret jug with a twisted rope handle which is in private possession in Bathgate. The oval panel is surrounded by elaborate engraved ornament of a Renaissance character and the quality of the glass and the general style would favour an attribution to John Ford. The matching goblet is engraved with a view of Donaldson's Hospital. A large goblet with an engraved view of Edinburgh Castle, the monogram TM and the date 1881, is in the Huntly House Museum, Edinburgh (Plate 52). Although the donor considered it to emanate

48 Celery glass with engraved decoration and ribbed handles, the design of the handles registered by Thomas Webb & Sons. 1867. h. $8^7/_8$ in. *Victoria & Albert Museum.*

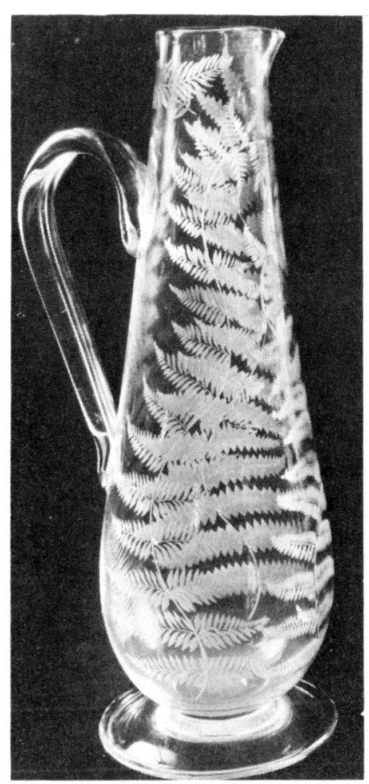

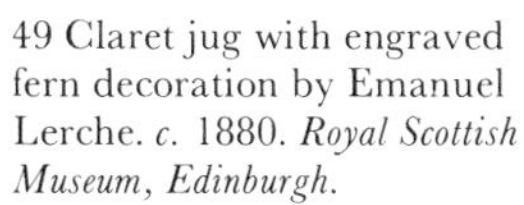

49 Claret jug with engraved fern decoration by Emanuel Lerche. *c.* 1880. *Royal Scottish Museum, Edinburgh.*

50 Goblet with an engraved view of the Royal Scottish Museum, Edinburgh, the Royal Arms and the initials 'V.R.'. On the stem is engraved 'MADE BY W. KEEDY IN PRESENCE OF PROFESSOR GEORGE WILSON AND HIS CLASS. HOLYROOD GLASS WORKS 1858'. Inside the knop, a Queen Victoria threepenny piece of 1858. h. $8^5/_8$ in. *Royal Scottish Museum, Edinburgh.*

51 Standing bowl engraved with a view of the Bathgate Academy and on the other side with the inscription 'Presented by James Brown to Grayshall Bowling Club Won by Archibald Fisher's rink 1870'. Made by the West Lothian Glass Works, Bathgate. 1870. h. 12 in. *Private collection.*

52 Goblet or standing bowl engraved with a view of Edinburgh Castle and wreaths of fern and flowers, monogram TM and date 1881, with coin in the base. Scottish (possibly Alexander Jenkinson, Norton Park). 1881. h. 12 in. *Huntly House Museum, Edinburgh.*

53 Goblet with a rural scene and the inscription 'The Mill the House the Miller – Where's his Donkey' in Gothic letters and with monogram 'WL' (for Walter Lindsay). Engraved by Emanuel Lerche at Alloa. *c.* 1880. *National Museum of Antiquities, Scotland.*

from the Holyrood Glass Works, the Museum is inclined to favour the firm of Alexander D. Jenkinson of Norton Park, Edinburgh, as the colour and quality of the glass are quite different from that of documented Holyrood specimens. Goblets with cut decoration and an etched (not engraved) view of Balmoral Castle were regularly ordered from John Ford by Queen Victoria as presents.

The large goblet illustrated in Plate 51 engraved with a view of the Bathgate Academy, was presented as a prize to the Grayshall Bowling Club, Bathgate, by James Brown in 1870 when it was won by Archibald Fisher's rink. It was made at the West Lothian Flint Glass Works at Bathgate, then a mining town midway between Glasgow and Edinburgh. This was evidently one of the more impressive pieces made by the glass-works which made all varieties of table glass, for both home and export trade. The speciality of the glass-works seems to have been fern engraving, particularly on wine glasses, a number of which survive. Many of the older inhabitants of Bathgate still speak affectionately of the 'fern glasses' that they remember from their childhood, although the existence of a flourishing glass-works has been largely forgotten.

The West Lothian Flint Glass Works was established by Donald Fraser (1802–69) in 1866. Donald Fraser had been a flint glass manufacturer in Edinburgh for a number of years firstly at 18

54 Claret jug inscribed with 'THE TOILETTE' after a painting by August Ludwig engraved by H. Burkner and published in the *Art Journal* in 1878. On the side of the jug, 'ENGRAVED BY WHYTE & SONS DUBLIN'. Made by Whyte & Sons, Dublin. c. 1878. h. 11½ in. *Victoria & Albert Museum.*

55 Magnum claret jug engraved with a view of the Alexandra Palace, London, and a dedicatory inscription to Sir Sills John Gibbons, Lord Mayor of London in 1872. Signed at base of handle 'Eng. by F. Eisert'. *Victoria & Albert Museum.*

56 & 57 Two claret jugs engraved by H. Keller for the Glasgow Glass Works of John Baird. *c.* 1886: Cupid, flowers and coronet. h. 12½ in. Apollo in his chariot. h. 12½ in. *Glasgow Museum & Art Gallery.*

Picardy Place, then at 33 Leith Walk and finally at 38 Leith Walk. In 1866, owing to extensive railway operations at Leith, Fraser was forced to vacate his works and seek premises elsewhere. He bought the Bathgate Old Brewery, in Chapel Lane, and proceeded to transform the building into a glass-works. The glass-works was in operation by May 1866, initially employing between fifty and sixty men. By 1871 it employed upwards of a 100, and by 1887, when the works closed down, there were 150. On the death of Donald Fraser in 1869 the glass-works was taken over by Messrs Wilson & Son of Glasgow. About 1884 the West Lothian Flint Glass Works again changed hands, this time being bought by Messrs James Couper & Sons of Glasgow, who changed the name to the Bathgate Glass Works. Couper's, who are perhaps best known for their 'Clutha' Glass (see Chapter 10) extended the range of products to include a good deal of coloured and fancy glass, but the works only survived for some three years and finally closed in 1887.

It is likely that most of these pictorially engraved pieces of Scottish glass (Plate 59) were the work of Bohemian immigrants for, apart from J. H. B. Millar, a number of other Bohemian and Central European engravers settled in Scotland. One of the best known was Emanuel Lerche who came to Edinburgh from Austria in 1853 and was first employed by Hauptmann & Company, glass-cutters, of 22 Greenside Place, Edinburgh. This firm was founded by Ignaz Hauptmann, a native of Bohemia who came to Edinburgh about 1837 and died there in 1887 at the age of sixty-nine. In 1861 Emanuel Lerche left Hauptmann and set up on his own at 7 Queen's Place, Edinburgh. In 1873, together with several of his workmen, he moved to the glass and pottery works of W. & J. A. Bailey at Alloa, where he remained until the works closed down in 1906. Following the closure he carried on as a freelance engraver. Lerche engraved many of the popular fern patterns (Plate 49), but he also engraved more elaborate, pictorial designs in typical Bohemian style, such as the 'Miller's Donkey' (Plate 53).

The names and addresses of a number of other Bohemian engravers working in Scotland are given in a sketchbook of Franz Tieze (also a Bohemian-born glass engraver), which is now in the Victoria & Albert Museum. One of them, F. J. Marschner, whose address is given as 22 South Back, Canongate, Edinburgh, possibly worked for John Ford, while another Marschner, possibly related, resided at

42 Alexandra Parade, Glasgow. Three other Glasgow-based engravers are listed: Vinzenz Austen, 243 Stirling Road, Glasgow; William Kleinpeter, 283 Harling Road; and Vincent Keller, whose address is given as James Couper's Flint Glass Works, Glasgow. Whether this is the same Keller employed by the Glasgow firm of James Baird in the 1870s and 1880s is not at present known. There are several examples of Baird's glass engraved by Keller in the collections of the Glasgow City Art Gallery, including a claret jug engraved with cupids and garlands (Plate 56), another with Apollo in his chariot riding over a dragon (Plate 57), and two claret jugs engraved with birds and elaborate foliage.

Franz Tieze himself came to England in 1862 at the age of twenty, a year after the death of his father who had been a schoolmaster. After three years in England, possibly in London, Tieze left on 28 January 1865 for Dublin, where, apart from several visits to Eng-

58 Goblet with cut stem and wheel-engraved decoration, on the bowl, of a view of a glasshouse inscribed 'Cottage Glass Works' with the royal arms and the initials J. & M. McL.'. Made at the Cottage Glass Works of John McLachlan & Co., William Street, Lambeth. *c.* 1860. h. 14 in. *Corning Museum of Glass, New York.*

land, and possibly Scotland, he spent the remainder of his working life engraving designs for the Pugh Glass Works in Potter's Alley. Most of the designs in Franz Tieze's sketchbook are typically Bohemian in style, with hunting scenes, stags and deer, and a couple of more exotic subjects of Arab steeds. A jug engraved by Tieze with deer in a characteristic Bohemian manner is in the Victoria & Albert Museum but his identified work in Dublin seems to have been specially adapted to Irish taste. His sketchbook contains the popular Irish motifs of the Irish wolfhound, the round tower, harp and shamrock with the inscription 'ERIN GO BRAGH.' A goblet with these motifs, in the collection of Mrs Thomas Pugh, is almost certainly from his hand, as is a claret jug (in the collection of Mrs Mary Boydell) which has typical late 1860s floral festoons corresponding to some of the drawings in his sketchbook. Another Bohemian engraver working in Dublin was Joseph Eisert, born in the same year as Tieze, who died in Dublin on 2 September 1871, at the early age of twenty-nine. The engraver of the fine William Whyte claret jug (Plate 54) was almost certainly a Bohemian, as yet unidentified as the piece is not signed. William Whyte were not manufacturers (although they had a financial interest in the Pugh Glass Works), but merchants who had a glass warehouse at 3/4 Marlborough Street, close to the Pughs. It is tempting to attribute the 'Toilette' jug to Tieze as his sketchbook contains sheets of Whyte's headed notepaper and he himself lived at 39 Marlborough Street. The subject is taken from an engraving of a painting by Auguste Ludwig, an engraving of which was published in the *Art Journal* of 1878. This is the subject of an article by Mrs Mary Boydell (who discovered the source of the design), in *Country Life* (6 May 1976). As Mrs Boydell points out it is most likely that the engraver would have copied the design from the plate in the *Art Journal*, which would almost certainly have been available in the Mechanics' Institute, which was practically next door to Whyte & Sons, and prided itself on containing a 'varied selection of newspapers, magazines, etc'.

Bohemian engravers were equally prominent in the Midlands, particularly in the Stourbridge area and in Birmingham. Once again several are listed by Franz Tieze. Among them was Francis Scheibner of Wordsley, who was employed by J. & J. Northwood, and Joseph Schiller, who lived at Broochmoor near Brierley Hill, and worked for Stevens & Williams. More is known of Joseph Keller, whose address is given by Tieze as 127 Great Tindel Street, Birmingham, although he is known to have worked for both Stevens and Williams, from about 1880 to 1925, and for Richardson's. The Brierley Hill Glass Museum possesses a volume of over 200 drawings, chiefly for glass engravings, which is entitled *A Collection of Patterns for the Use of Glass Decorators, Designed by Joseph Keller*. The volume is undated, but was probably produced about 1885, and contains several designs for the rock crystal style which are described as 'polished bright'. Some of the designs were engraved by Keller himself for Stevens & Williams, while some were carried out by other engravers, including John Orchard, an English engraver who worked at Stevens & Williams from the mid-1880s. Whether Joseph Keller was related to the Scottish-based Kellers is not known, but two families of Bohemian engravers, the Fritsches and the Knys, settled in the Stourbridge area. They were most prominent in the rock crystal style and their work is discussed later in this chapter.

In the south many of the most prominent glass engravers were also immigrants. One of the most skilled was Paul Oppitz, the son of George Oppitz, himself a glass engraver, and Josepha Oppitz, who was a glass improver. Paul Oppitz was born at Haida, near Prague, on 24 June 1827, and in 1843, at the age of eighteen, he came to London, living first at Stamford Street, Blackfriars, and later at 38 John Street, Blackfriars Road. He became a naturalised British subject in 1853 and three years later married Sarah Holland, moving to 23 John Street. Several years later he moved again to 22 Vardens Road, Clapham Junction, where his most important work was carried out, much of it commissioned by Copeland's in the 1870s and 1880s. The Copeland glass vase (Plate 60) was exhibited at the Vienna Exhibition of 1873, and was awarded a Bronze Medal. Apparently it took Paul Oppitz 243 days to engrave the vase, which was purchased by Sir Richard Wallace and subsequently acquired by the Victoria & Albert Museum. The original design, which is in the style of the arabesques of Berain, was by J. Jones, an artist employed by Copeland's. The tracing from which Oppitz worked still exists and a comparison of the tracing and the finished engraving shows that some latitude was given to the engraver for some additional fine detail has been added and the winged beasts do not appear in the original tracing. Apart from the Copeland vase, a number of pieces by Paul Oppitz are still in his family's possession,

59 Jug with ribbed handle and engraved decoration by Alexander B. Miller. John Ford, Holyrood Glass Works, Edinburgh, probably *c.* 1880. h. 10$^{1}/_{8}$ in. *City Museum, Edinburgh.*

60 Two-handled vase with wheel-engraved decoration designed by J. Jones and engraved by Franz Oppitz for Copeland's. Exhibited at the Vienna Exhibition of 1873 and awarded a bronze medal. *Victoria & Albert Museum.*

including a standing cup with views of Stolzenfels and Rheinstein, an amber-coloured covered goblet, which received a Silver Medal at the Turners' Competition of 1887, and several more modest pieces including carafes and wine glasses in a variety of styles. Paul Oppitz died in 1894 at the age of sixty-seven. Another London-based Bohemian engraver was Franz Eisert (possibly related to Joseph Eisert of Dublin), who had a workshop at 25 South Audley Street, and later, in 1872, at 3 Grafton Street, Fitzroy Square. A magnum claret jug (Plate 55), now in the Victoria & Albert Museum, engraved by Eisert with a view of the Alexandra Palace, was presented to Sir Sills John Gibbons, Lord Mayor of London, in 1872.

Having discussed the work of some of the known immigrant engravers, it is now time to turn to a more general examination of styles in engraved glass, including the work of some native-born engravers.

A study of the glass shown at the Paris Exhibition of 1867 shows that in the five years since the London International Exhibition the demand for engraved table glass had increased considerably. Once again the London dealers were prominent in this field and the Classical or Greek style continued in favour, together with other historic styles such as Italian Renaissance and Medieval. The Artisan Reports of the 1867 Paris Exhibition, published by the Society of Arts, contain a report by a Mr W. T. Swene, described as the practical superintendent of a Birmingham glass-works. Mr Swene remarks that 'the study of the various forms to be met with in the floral world and their application to art workmanship has been forgotten in the demand for historic art'. However, a number of firms, notably the London ones, did include water sets engraved with festoons of ivy, and the fern patterns also continued. A Richardson pattern book of the late 1860s, and a John Ford pattern book of approximately the same date, include a number of such engraved natural patterns, and also other designs of festoons or swags of flowers, often combined with historic ornament or with birds.

This predeliction for eclectic, historical styles continued in the 1870s and the scope of inspiration increased. The Report of the Paris Exhibition of 1878 by Joseph Leicester (whose own work is discussed in Chapter 8), published by the Society of Arts, confirms this view. In his general remarks on engraving Joseph Leicester also remarks on the lack of floral decoration:

> Some of the exhibits were adorned with battle scenes, figure piled upon figure, so overcrowded that the work appeared like dull stone. Wherever the observer turned he was met by the classical head, the classical form, the classical figure, the classical robes, as if there was no room in the world for anything else but classical forms, and an endless repetition of the same subject. I confess to having become very tired of this, and to have considered why the floral world had not been drawn upon by the artists for more varied and not less beautiful and effective subjects, eminently adapted for ornamentation on glass.

Although the Classical style still predominated at the 1878 Exhibition, other historic styles were not neglected and Arabian, Assyrian, Byzantine, Egyptian, Persian, Indian, Chinese, and Japanese, Celtic and Medieval, Renaissance and even eighteenth-century styles all found their expression in engraving on glass. Indeed, as the *Pottery Gazette* (July 1878), put it, 'every style known to South Kensington' was applied to table glass. The Thomas Webb exhibit in 1878, for which the firm was awarded a Gold Medal, covered the entire range. An examination of the pattern books of Stevens & Williams at this

61 Claret jug and stopper with wheel-engraved decoration, probably by James O'Fallon, and patent drip ring. Made by Philip Pargeter, Red House Glass Works, Stourbridge, registered 20 May 1874. Base etched with diamond registration mark and 'P. JONES WESTMORLAND STREET DUBLIN'. h. $9^1/_4$ in. *Private collection.*

62 The 'Elgin' vase with etched decoration and a band of relief carving by John Northwood. Commissioned by J. B. (later Sir Benjamin) Stone *c.* 1865 and completed in 1873. h. $15^1/_2$ in. *City Museum & Art Gallery, Birmingham.*

period shows that Webb's were not alone in this eclecticism, which was widespread throughout the trade. At Thomas Webb's, the Artistic Director, James O'Fallon, himself a skilled engraver capable of executing work in any style (Plate 61), was responsible for much of the engraved glass shown at Paris. It was perhaps natural that O'Fallon, an Irishman, should excel at the Celtic style. Joseph Leicester describes his Celtic service as being like 'poems moulded into glass'. The bowls of the glasses were pear-shaped, with double twisted stems, made very pure and light with very delicate lines and curves interlaced into each other in the most easy and flowing manner. There were also Celtic decanters, claret jugs and vases, some of them with 'rock crystal' engraving, which is described later in this chapter. Reviewing the exhibit the *European Mail Supplement* (1 October 1878), writes of the sources of inspiration: 'The illuminations in the Book of Kells, the Book of Armagh; the pattern, line within line, involution within involution, on such works as the Bell of St Patrick, the Tara Brooch and the Harp of Brian Boroimhe, all these are an evangel of art in themselves to one willing to accept and bale to grasp their meaning. That Mr O'Fallon has fully imbued himself with their spirit is proved beyond cavil.'

63 The 'Pegasus' or 'Dennis' vase with cameo decoration by John Northwood. Commissioned by Thomas Wilkes Webb about 1876 and completed in 1882. h. $21^1/_2$ in. *Smithsonian Institute, Washington.*

64 Cameo vase 'Raising an altar to Bacchus' decorated by Alphonse Lecheverel for Hodgetts, Richardson & Son, Stourbridge, and probably shown at the Paris Exhibition of 1878. h. $15^5/_8$ in. *Brierley Hill Collection.*

One of O'Fallon's most important works is a large crystal vase or flagon, of a flattened discoid shape, carved in Egyptian style. On the front is a mask, from which radiate stems of papyrus, with a winged insect below, while the reverse is carved with a sunburst with a curiously shaped boat below. The sides are decorated with scarabs alternating with panels of basketwork. O'Fallon worked for two years on the vase but it remained unfinished and it was taken, many years later, in its unmounted state, to the Athenaeum Club in London, by a member, Mr Alfred Percival Graves. It was then mounted in silver and became the subject of a letter or petition to the Prime Minister, signed by a number of prominent members of the

65 Cameo glass vase designed and executed by Thomas and George Woodall for Thomas Webb & Sons, Stourbridge. *c.* 1890. Signed in the cameo 'T. & G. Woodall' and 'Psyche Thomas Webb & Sons' etched on base. h. 10¼ in. *Philadelphia Museum of Art.*

club. This resulted in a gratuity of £100 to O'Fallon, which he received in 1919. The whereabouts of the flagon remained unknown until it was sold, as part of an extensive private collection, at Phillips, Son & Neale in April, 1976.

The sources of O'Fallon's inspiration were not, however, always so lofty and he was the perpetrator of a number of grotesque and humorous designs of animals, often anthropomorphically treated. These included a tankard engraved with eight frogs in different postures imitating *homo sapiens*, a pilgrim bottle illustrating the Darwinian theory of evolution with tadpoles and frogs on tight ropes, a vase with a pig and another with an irate cat being taunted by a cock. The *Queen* (7 September 1878), in reviewing these frivolities, somewhat pompously states that 'the spirit of Jerome Bosche, the whimsical, and Peter Breughel, the droll, of sixteenth-century memory, has been revived indeed by Mr O'Fallon's grotesque humour'.

This grotesque style was evidently popular and remained in favour throughout the 1880s, being reflected in styles of enamelled and pressed glass, as well as in engraving. Frogs also seem to have been a speciality with a London engraver, John Lloyd Burleton, who was born about 1820, and had a glass-engraving workshop at 4 Wilmington Street, Wilmington Square from 1852 to 1894. He was already a glass engraver, then working in Tichfield Street, when he married in 1842. His son, Charles Burleton, born in 1857, was also a glass engraver who worked with his father at Wilmington Street. Later, Charles Burleton had a glass and engraving shop at the Crystal Palace in Sydenham and in the 1898 London Directory he

66 Three cameo vases designed by Frederick Carder for Stevens and Williams. *c*. 1885. *Corning Museum of Glass, New York*.

appears as a china and glass dealer at 194 Tulse Hill. Several pieces of glass engraved by the Burletons remain in the family's possession. They include a tumbler with a frog, which is a very skilled piece of engraving and was probably engraved by John Lloyd Burleton in the late 1870s, as was the heron tumbler, both of which show a distinct Japanese influence. There is also a large jug similarly engraved with butterflies, blossom and grasses, and a small wine glass with Egyptian-style ornament.

Apart from these historic and exotic styles, throughout the 1860s, 1870s and 1880s, appropriate patterns were engraved on table glass especially for the Christmas trade. This is particularly noticeable in the pattern books of Stevens & Williams, where such designs occur every year in the late autumn. The patterns include wreaths of mistletoe and ivy, wreaths of holly, a robin on an ivy bough encircled by holly, or a turkey with holly and mistletoe. Such patterns occur on claret jugs and decanters and on tazzas and comports.

In the late 1870s, a new and distinctive style of glass-engraving emerged, a style which provided a rich and elegant method of decoration for table glass, lamps and purely ornamental objects. Its chief characteristic was that the engraved areas and lines were polished so that the whole area of the vessel was uniformly bright, whereas with normal wheel-engraving the engraved areas were left

67 Cameo vase in two layers of glass, the outer pink, the inner green, the outer layer cut in a Persian-style floral design. Designed by T. Woodall and executed by W. Hill for Thomas Webb & Sons, Stourbridge. 1884. Exhibited at the International Health Exhibition of 1884. h. $6^5/_8$ in. *Victoria & Albert Museum.*

68 Vase in 'rock crystal' style made by Thomas Webb & Sons, Stourbridge. The base bears an etched mark 'WEBB' in a decorative cartouche. *c.* 1890. h. 8 in. *Philadelphia Museum of Art.*

unpolished to contrast with the surrounding bright areas. The engraving on the 'rock crystal' pieces was much deeper than in normal wheel-engraving and tended to be used over almost the whole surface of the vessel. It had the appearance of carving rather than engraving and as such was akin to cameo decoration which evolved about the same time.

According to an article by James O'Fallon in the *Art Journal* for 1885, the style arose in France about 1877 or 1878. The French glass engravers then began to display a marked departure from the current formal styles of engraving, adopting a freer style much influenced by the spirit of Japanese design. The Baccarat factory specialised in this new, polished rock crystal engraving and a number of French firms, including the Cristallerie de Pantin and the dealer *A L'Escalier de Cristal* showed rock crystal at the Paris Exhibition of 1878, described by the *Art Journal Catalogue* as decorated with 'bold floral patterns, with birds and other objects, in this deep engraving which is brilliantly polished'. Although O'Fallon implies that it was a French innovation, this polished engraving seems to have developed spontaneously in England at approximately the same time as in France. Indeed, O'Fallon himself was responsible for an elaborate pair of claret jugs in Celtic style, each with a handle in the form of a grotesque monster, one of which is illustrated in the *Art Journal* article by O'Fallon and is described as partly etched and then engraved and polished with very small wheels. These jugs were exhibited by Thomas Webb at the Paris Exhibition of 1878 and purchased by Sir Richard Wallace. Soon after this several English

69 'Rock crystal' bowl with Chinese symbols. Designed by John Northwood and engraved by Frank Scheibner for Stevens & Williams, Brierley Hill. 1884. diam. $10^5/_8$ in. *Victoria & Albert Museum.*

firms, notably Thomas Webb and Stevens & Williams took up rock crystal engraving on an intensive scale. The words 'rock crystal' first appear in Thomas Webb's pattern books applied to a set of table glass engraved by Frederick E. Kny with animal scenes. The first mention of 'rock crystal' in Stevens & Williams's pattern books occurs in January 1880 (no. 5740) with a thumbnail sketch of a two-handled vase with cut pillars and flower engraving in a somewhat Japanese style. Indeed, this Far Eastern influence is apparent in most of the rock crystal designs which usually consisted of trailing sprays of Japanese-style blossom and birds or chinoiserie designs of chrysanthemums and scrolling ornament. The shapes themselves are often reminiscent of Chinese jades or early bronzes and, as in the case of the bowl illustrated in Plate 69, designed by John Northwood and engraved by Frank Scheibner, the Chinese character '*shou*' (for longevity) was incorporated into the design. The use of a Japanese style can be seen as an expression of the general Japanese influence that was an essential part of the 'aesthetic' movement affecting most of the decorative arts in the late 1870s and 1880s. It was, however, a more sophisticated expression of the Japanese style than that prevailing in the contemporary printed earthenware or wallpapers and fabrics in the normal run of commercial production.

The production of these sophisticated rock crystal pieces formed a considerable part of the production of Thomas Webb and Stevens &

70 'Rock crystal' bowl engraved with carp amid waves. Impressed WEBB trademark under foot. Made by George Woodall for Thomas Webb & Sons. 1890. h. $3^{3}/_{8}$ in. *Private collection.*

Williams (and to a lesser extent of that of Stuart & Sons of the Red House Glass Works) during the 1880s and 1890s. Most of this work was carried out by immigrant Bohemian engravers, but James O'Fallon was also responsible for a number of pieces. Although at that time O'Fallon was Art Director at Thomas Webb's, he appears to have also worked freelance for Stevens & Williams. A series of claret jugs, engraved in the 'rock crystal' technique with flowers and birds (including two rather comic baby ducks) is marked as having been engraved by O'Fallon and dated 26 February 1880. The main resident engraver of rock crystal at Stevens & Williams was a Bohemian, Joseph Keller, and a notable exhibit of his rock crystal was shown by the firm at the Wolverhampton Exhibition of 1884.

At Thomas Webb's the most prominent engravers in this style were again of Bohemian origin – Frederick Englebert Kny and William Fritsche, both of whom had their own workshops at the firm. Frederick Kny worked for a short time at James Powell & Sons, before joining Thomas Webb's, where he worked until his death about 1900. William Fritsche was born in a small village in Bohemia about 1853 and came to England about 1868 where he joined Thomas Webb as an engraver. He worked there for almost fifty years and died on 24 March 1924. One of Fritsche's most ambitious pieces of rock crystal is a large jug (now in the Corning Museum of Glass) which is in a late Renaissance or Baroque style and which, with its gadrooning, scroll work and mask, seems to have been inspired by continental silverwork. Most of the rock crystal produced by Thomas Webb's, whether under the direction of Fritsche or Kny, is in Oriental style. It includes decanters and goblets engraved with phoenix and Chinese ornament or Chinese dragons. Other designs of the mid-1880s have chrysanthemums or Chinese floral and scrolling ornament, sometimes set in scrolling panels with a somewhat swirling movement. An elaborate rock crystal toilet set by Thomas Webb, dated 1886, is engraved in this manner. It also includes several designs of carp and waves, among them the small bowl (illustrated in Plate 70) which has tiny fish engraved behind the bosses. This bowl corresponds to a design in Webb's pattern books (no. 18082), 'flint carved RC' (rock crystal) and the price book records 'bowl flint carved w2499 Mar 19.90. h. 3³/₈". It is unusual in that it is by George Woodall, who is not usually associated with 'rock crystal' but is well-known for his work in cameo. Many of the rock crystal pieces were first cut in pillars and the trailing floral decoration cut across the edges of the pillars. This is characteristic of the freedom of 'rock crystal' and gives a spontaneity to the design which is often lacking in normally engraved pieces (Plates 70, 71 and 72).

The fullest account to date of the 'rock crystal' style is given in the catalogue of an exhibition of 'English Rock Crystal Glass 1878–1925' held at Dudley Art Gallery in 1976.

At Stuart and Sons the main engraver of rock crystal was Ludwig Kny, the son of Frederick. Ludwig Kny trained for three years in Paris and also studied at South Kensington. He was a skilled engraver, especially of hunting scenes, but also executed rock crystal engraving and some cameo glass. He first worked at Webb's but joined Stuart & Sons as a designer some time in the 1880s. A number of his designs for rock crystal appear in Stuart & Sons' pattern books from 1887 onwards. They are very similar to the designs produced by Thomas Webb and Stevens & Williams and include patterns of almond blossom, peacocks, sparrows and other birds, fish and seaweed in the current Japanese style, together with two more distinctive patterns with rococo scrolls and leaves and a cupid and flowers.

Another sophisticated method of glass decoration was 'intaglio'

71 Three examples of 'rock crystal' glass: Wine glass by Thomas Webb. *c.* 1905. h. 6$^1/_8$ in. Covered jar engraved by Joseph Keller for Stevens & Williams, mid 1880s. h. 9$^1/_8$ in. Decanter and stopper engraved by William Fritsche for Thomas Webb & Sons. *c.* 1897. h. 13$^5/_8$ in. All in the makers' possession. *Photograph Victoria & Albert Museum.*

engraving, developed mainly by John Northwood, who was Art Director at Stevens & Williams from the early 1880s until his death in 1902. John Northwood was born in 1836, his father being the owner of a village grocery shop in Glass House Hill, Wordsley. From an early age he showed a marked talent for drawing and at the age of twelve he was apprenticed to the firm W. H., B. & J. Richardson to learn the art of painting, gilding and enamelling. For a short while, during the re-organisation of the firm, he worked for his brother William who was a builder. When the works re-opened under Benjamin Richardson, he rejoined the firm, working together with Thomas Bott, W. J. Muckley (who was to become Art Master at Manchester School of Art), Philip Pargeter and others who were to become leading figures in the Stourbridge glass industry. Northwood attended classes at the Stourbridge School of Art and was awarded a Bronze Medal at the age of eighteen in 1855. He also taught at the school for a while. He set up his own workshops in 1859 and it was not until 1881 or 1882 that he joined Stevens & Williams as Art Director and Works Manager.

Intaglio engraving, which can be considered as midway between engraving and cutting, was carried out with small stone wheels used

72 'Rock crystal' glass bowl, engraved with fish and aquatic plants. Signed 'William Fritsche' and made by Thomas Webb & Sons, Stourbridge. *c.* 1885. diam. 9 in. *Sotheby's Belgravia.*

in place of the copper wheels on the engraver's lathe. It produced deep engraved lines and small cuts which could be polished (giving a somewhat similar effect to 'rock crystal') or left unpolished. It could be combined successfully with normal cut decoration. Full details of the technical process are given in *John Northwood* by John Northwood II (Stourbridge, 1958). 'Intaglio' engraving (or 'tag', as it was affectionately called by the workers) first came into use about 1892 and by the end of the century it accounted for a considerable part of the output of Stevens & Williams and was adopted by other Stourbridge firms. Apart from John Northwood, Joshua Hodgetts was much concerned with the perfection of this technique. 'Intaglio' engraving was generally employed for rather delicate floral patterns or scrolling designs – often in art nouveau style (Plate 73) and was particularly suitable for the decoration of table glass, especially wine glasses, goblets, claret jugs and decanters.

John Northwood's most spectacular contribution was the revival of 'cameo glass', often regarded as the most remarkable achievement

73 Vase of pale green glass layered with pinkish glass, the design produced by intaglio cutting. Marked 'Stevens & Williams 1901'. h. 12 in. *Victoria & Albert Museum.*

of British glass-works in the late nineteenth century. British glass-makers had long admired the celebrated Portland Vase in the British Museum but no one had so far had the audacity to essay the same technique. *The Magazine of Art* (vol. X, 1887, p. 187 *et seq.*), in an article on cameo glass entitled 'A Lost Art Revived', remarks that one of the strangest phenomena in the history of art has been 'the way in which one special branch of art will bud in existence in some country, blossom to its full maturity, remain for some time in the perfection of its fruition, then wither to decadence, and ultimately entirely decay'. Such an art was cameo glass, which, having been 'a lost art for a thousand or fifteen hundred years . . . has been revived, and so successfully revived as to take its place among the first favourites of modern art manufacture'. John Northwood was the first to essay the lost technique of cameo glass carving, although his first step in that direction was not strictly speaking cameo, which implies a vessel made of one shade of glass, cased with an outer layer of opaque white glass which is carved away to leave white decoration in relief. His first achievement in the direction of cameo was his 'Elgin' vase (Plate 62), the completion of which occupied his spare time for some nine years. It was commissioned in 1864 by Sir Benjamin Stone and was made in clear crystal glass at the Birmingham works of Stone, Fawdry and Stone. It was of Classical Greek form with two curved, crook-shaped handles, and the main decoration was a relief carved frieze of horsemen copied from the Elgin Marbles in the British Museum, with subsidiary bands of Greek ornament executed by acid-etching. It was finally completed in 1873. This was followed by a commission from his cousin Philip Pargeter (then owner of the Red House Glass Works) for a copy of the Portland Vase. After several attempts a good and accurate blank was made (said to have been made by Daniel Hancock). Northwood was asked to complete the replica for a sum in the region of one thousand pounds. He worked on this replica for three years, travelling many times to the British Museum to compare his work with the original and it was finally completed in 1876. It was shown at the Paris Exhibition of 1878 on the stand of R. P. Daniell, the London dealer. One of the results of this achievement was that Northwood was approached by Josiah Wedgwood & Sons to execute the cutting and polishing on some of their Jasper ware reproductions of the Portland Vase which he did during the years 1877–9. At his Wordsley workshop some of his engravers and etchers also decorated a considerable quantity of Wedgwood 'Rockingham' ware.

The manufacture of cameo glass presented considerable technical difficulties. The basic steps of the process are as follows. The glass-blower dips the end of his tube into a pot of molten glass of the colour which is to form the body; this gather is then marvered to a convenient shape; it is then dipped into a roughly shaped cup of semi-molten glass of the colour of the decoration (if three colours or layers are required the operation is repeated). The gather of glass is then reheated so that the different parts become firmly fused together. It is then blown to the required shape, and after annealing and tempering the blank is ready for the decorator. The chief difficulty was to get the different layers of colour of such a make that they would expand and contract equally and it sometimes happened that a completed piece would 'fly' in the workshop if it was exposed to any sudden change of temperature. The first process was to deaden the bright surface of the glass by immersing it in a bath of acid. The basic design was then drawn in a bituminous varnish which would resist hydrofluoric acid. The piece was then placed in a bath of hydro-

74 Tumbler with diamond-point engraving of three royal coats of arms and the inscriptions 'Thurso 26 May 1863' and 'Isabella MacKay 1863'. Unsigned, but probably by the engraver T. Sutherland. h. 4¼ in. *Private collection.*

75 Rummer with diamond-point engraving of royal coats of arms, a doggerel verse and other devices, signed 'T. Sutherland' and dated 1847. In the possession of Delomosne & Sons in 1967. h. 5 in. *Photograph Victoria & Albert Museum.*

fluoric acid which ate away the outer layer except where it had been protected by the varnish. With the basic design in relief, the piece was ready for carving by hand, although some of the less intricate parts of the design could be executed with an engraving wheel. Minute engraving tools – such as those used in gem engraving – were used for the finer details.

Philip Pargeter was so delighted with the copy of the Portland Vase that he commissioned Northwood to produce an original design in cameo. This was the 'Milton' vase, which appeared on the stand of James Green & Nephew at the Paris Exhibition of 1878. The subject, taken from Milton's *Paradise Lost*, shows the expulsion of Adam and Eve from the Garden of Eden by the archangel Michael. Following the Milton Vase, three cameo tazzas were completed by Northwood for Pargeter, each about nine inches in diameter and representing Art, Literature and Science, with medallion portraits of Flaxman, Shakespeare and Newton. There was to have been a third – James Watt representing Engineering – but this was not executed, although the pencil sketch for the portrait still exists.

In the mid-1870s Thomas Wilkes Webb, Director of Thomas Webb's, also became interested in Northwood's work and, not to be outdone, commissioned from him the 'Pegasus' or 'Dennis' vase, now in the Smithsonian Museum, Washington (Plate 63). This covered vase stands twenty-two inches high and is of a deep rich blue with the decoration in semi-opaque white glass. The cover is surmounted by Pegasus, the winged horse, and the heads of two seahorses form the handles. On the body, carved in relief, are: on one side Amphitrite and Cupid, preceded by a triton and accompanied by nereids and seahorses; on the reverse Aurora, Goddess of the Dawn, in her chariot, surrounded by cupids. This vase, in an unfinished state, was also shown at the Paris Exhibition of 1878 on the Webb stand, and was no doubt a contributory factor in the firm's award of the Grand Prix for glass. The vase was completed in 1882.

Cameo work was also shown at the Paris Exhibition by Richardson's, mainly executed by the French medallist Alphonse Eugene Lecheverel, who worked in England for only a few years. The vase illustrated in Plate 64 was probably shown at Paris. The Richardson exhibit also included an unfinished copy of the Portland Vase by Joseph Locke (who had worked with Northwood) and who later went to the United States.

By the 1880s cameo was being produced on a commercial scale, mostly decorative vases and small items such as scent bottles. Cameo featured prominently at the International Health Exhibition of 1884 and five Webb pieces were bought by the South Kensington Museum (now the Victoria & Albert Museum).

Thomas Webb and Stevens & Williams were the leading producers of cameo glass, although Richardson's produced a considerable quantity of what may be termed commercial cameo, not embarking on the more ambitious figure subjects (apart from those produced by Lecheverel and Locke). Most of the more modest pieces were decorated with floral patterns – poppies and grasses, sunflowers, chrysanthemums, irises, anemones and a host of other flowers (Plate 58), or with fruit and berries – or with formal patterns in Indian or Persian style (Plate 67). These commercial pieces were not carved in such high relief as the outer casing of white glass was much thinner and by the use of the engraving wheel the modelling was executed much more quickly.

At Stevens & Williams the most important cameo blanks were made by Tom Cartwright who was an expert glass-maker. After John Northwood became Art Director there the decorating firm of J. & J. Northwood worked extensively on cameo for Stevens & Williams. There was a large staff of experienced decorators, including William Northwood, James Hill, Frank Scheibner, Joshua Hodgetts and Benjamin Fenn.

At Thomas Webb's, the brothers Thomas and George Woodall, who had originally been employed by J. & J. Northwood, were in charge of the cameo workshops. George Woodall, in particular, developed his own personal style of figure work which was less classical than Northwood's and more contemporary in feeling, having a slightly frivolous quality that was in tune with the spirit of the 'gay nineties' (Plate 65). The well-known 'Moorish Bathers' plaque is typical of his style, with the subtle graduation of depth to indicate the transparency of the fluttering draperies.

The commercial success and popularity of English cameo led various Bohemian firms to imitate the effect by painting designs in white enamel in varying thicknesses to give the effect of low relief decoration. These Bohemian imitations, which could be executed very cheaply, can give a fairly credible effect at a first glance but the difference is detected quite clearly on inspection.

A different effect in cameo glass at Stevens & Williams was achieved by a coloured casing on a light coloured body. The relief design was then executed in the colour and the body ground was 'peckled' or 'chipped' all over. Another production of Stevens & Williams, that was somewhat akin to cameo, was '*Dolce Relievo*'. This glass had an ivory body and a coloured casing, usually green or light purple, which was decorated by etching in low relief.

Diamond point engraving does not appear to have been practised extensively during the Victorian period, certainly not on a commercial scale. It seems to have been carried out by individual craftsmen, using blanks from various glass-houses, probably to order for special commissions, often for commemorative purposes.

An interesting group of diamond point engraved rummers and tumblers with similar pictorial motifs and varying inscriptions has a range of date from 1847 to 1863. The stylistic affinity between the engraving of the motifs and written inscriptions on all the glasses points to an attribution to a single, as yet unidentified engraver. Another common factor is that all the glasses bear versions of the Royal Coats of Arms, each treated with the same stylistic idiosyn-

76 & 77 Two views of a rummer with capstan stem and plain foot, diamond-point engraved with a variety of motifs including the royal coat of arms, a hackney carriage, a ship, farm implements, a fox, a stag, Queen Victoria on horseback, Windsor Castle, a coach and four, a paddle steamer and doggerel verses. Signed 'Sutherland' and dated 'London, 1854'. h. $5^{1}/_{8}$ in. *Victoria & Albert Museum.*

crasies. The earliest dated glass of the group, a rummer which belonged to Delomosne (the London glass dealers) in 1967 has two coats of arms and other devices with a doggerel verse and is signed 'T. Sutherland' and dated 1847 (Plate 75). Another glass signed 'Sutherland, London' with the Royal Coat of Arms and scenes of hunting and shooting, inscribed 'To Mrs Rogers by J. Crofts 2nd Life Guards 1853' was sold at Sotheby's in 1963. A third example signed 'Sutherland, London' again with the Royal Coat of Arms, Queen Victoria on horseback, a railway engine, coach and horses, and inscribed 'E.H. 1854. Forget me not', is in the Victoria & Albert Museum (Plates 76, 77), together with a similar unsigned example. Leicester Museum also has two similar rummers. Other unsigned glasses with Windsor Castle, Whitehall, Royal arms and doggerel verses, obviously from the same hand, were illustrated in an advertisement by Cecil Davis in the *Burlington Magazine* in 1925, and two examples, one with the inscription 'W. H. Hislop 1850 to Chas. Dickens'. A tumbler with three coats of arms, the date 1851 and some verses, is illustrated by Sidney Crompton in his book *English Glass* (London, 1967) and other examples have turned up in various sale catalogues. The latest dated example traced so far is the tumbler illustrated in Plate 74, which bears the inscription 'Isabella Mackay 1863' and is dated 'Thurso 26 May 1863'. From this evidence it is tempting to assume that Sutherland was an engraver who worked in London in the late 1840s and 1850s and moved to Scotland in the late 1850s or early 1860s. Although the Sutherland of these glasses has at some time been identified with the well-known engraver Thomas Sutherland, this cannot be the case, for apart from the fact that Sutherland's work is far too professional and sophisticated, he died in 1838 before the first glass was engraved.

CHAPTER 7

ETCHED GLASS

ACID-ETCHING was an extremely popular method of decorating table glass in the second half of the nineteenth century. In its simplest form, the process consisted of covering the surface of the glass which was to be decorated with an acid-resisting substance such as wax (usually a beeswax and resin mixture). The desired pattern was then incised through the wax with a steel-pointed stiletto. The whole object was then dipped in hydrofluoric acid, which ate into the glass where it had been exposed by the stiletto.

Another method was to take designs in the form of transfers in acid-resisting printing ink, from an engraved plate, and to fix them to the object, which was then subjected to the acid bath. A third method was to paint a design on the glass with a bituminous acid-resisting paint. The object was then immersed in the acid bath which attacked all areas not protected by the paint. This was the first stage in making the commercial cameo glass when the painted design would be left in relief.

The credit for the first commercially successful application of the acid-etching process is generally given to Thomas Hawkes of Dudley, where gold enamelled glass plates were ornamented by etching by a Mr Wainwright and others. In 1835 this firm produced a large plateau with engraved and etched decoration by William Herbert, a member of a Dudley family of glass engravers. This plateau, which was silver mounted, was presented to the Hon. Spring Rice (later Lord Monteagle) but it is no longer in the family's possession and does not appear to have survived. Although other Midland glass factories employed this technique in the late 1830s and 1840s, until the middle of the century the process was still at an experimental stage. Its subsequent development undoubtedly owed much to Benjamin Richardson who had begun his career in the Thomas Hawkes glass-works. In the mid-1850s, when he was in charge of the Richardson firm, he spent some time perfecting the process to a viable commercial proposition. In 1857, Benjamin Richardson took out a patent to protect his discoveries. The essence of this patent was the addition of sulphuric acid to the hydrofluoric acid, in order to produce a bright etched finish, together with the use of gutta-percha, or india-rubber, as the protecting cover. The patent also covered the use of hydrofluoric acid for etching through layered glass, as in a goblet, which is inscribed 'Mr B. Richardson, Wordsley, 1857' (the year of the patent). In this work he was assisted by John Northwood and T. Guest. Two years later, in 1859, John Northwood, together with his brother Joseph, H. G. Richardson and T. Guest, set up a decorating business at the lower end of Barnet Lane, Wordsley. The buildings included an etching room, an acidising shop, a plant for making hydrofluoric acid and a warehouse. The workshops were fully in operation by 1860, but the following year the partnership was dissolved and John and Joseph carried on the business as J. & J. Northwood. A wide variety of etched patterns was executed, mainly floral in character, often combined with ferns, grasses, birds and butterflies. Pictorial and ornamental designs were also carried out, in the current styles found on engraved glass, including Greek and Roman ornament with classical figures, Renaissance designs and others with Egyptian motifs. John Northwood built up an extensive library of art books and periodicals, books of ornament such as Owen Jones's *Grammar of Ornament* (London, 1856) which was almost the 'bible' for the Victorian designer in all fields of the decorative arts.

Northwood gathered round him a team of workers, most of whom were trained at the Stourbridge School of Art including the Woodall brothers (who became renowned for their cameo glass), Benjamin Fenn, Joshua Hodgetts, Albert Gyngell (who became a well-known landscape artist) and Harry Northwood, who later emigrated to the United States where he became famous for his iridescent pressed glass, now known as 'carnival glass'. One of the most talented etchers at the Northwood workshops was James Hill, who, when a

78 Goblet, clear glass with geometric etched decoration. Bought from W. P. & G. Phillips & Pearce. 1871. h. 4 in. *Kunstgewerbemuseum, Berlin.*

79 Champagne jug with template-etched decoration. *c.* 1868. Probably by John Northwood. h. 9¼ in. *Private collection.*

student at the Stourbridge School of Art, won many prizes in the National Art Students Competitions at South Kensington. A number of his drawings survive, in the family's possession, finely executed designs in the whole gamut of current styles.

John Northwood himself drew a great deal of inspiration from specimens of historic glass in museum collections, notably in the British Museum and the South Kensington Museum. He also visited

80 Rummer of clear glass with acid-etched decoration marked 'Patent Etching and Ornamental Glass Company, Globe Works, Sheffield'. Mid-19th century. h. 5 in. *Victoria & Albert Museum.*

Paris to study the glass in the Louvre and the Cluny Museum. Northwood's contribution to the development of etching was not, however, only in the field of design; even more important were his technical innovations.

The first of these was the template etching machine, first used in 1861. Details of this machine are given in John Northwood II's book on his father (*John Northwood: His Contribution to the Stourbridge Flint Glass Industry*, Stourbridge, 1958). By means of this machine, patterns could be produced with great precision, patterns that equalled, or even excelled in delicacy the patterns produced more laboriously, and expensively, by hand-engraving. A typical example of a pattern produced by template etching is shown in Plate 79. The templates – a kind of stencil – were mostly cut out of tin foil, but those for the more popular patterns, which would be used many times, were cut from tin plate, or thin brass or copper sheets.

Northwood's next innovation was the geometrical etching machine, the first full-size workable model being developed in about 1865. The machine was somewhat similar to a lathe and was worked by a hand wheel. The movements consisted of circular actions achieved by means of trains of wheels in conjunction with various shaped cams and levers. The patterns executed by it were repeating patterns, the earliest and most popular patterns being those known as the 'key' pattern (a Greek key design) and the 'Circle' (a continuous band of overlapping circles). These patterns were much used for the bowls of wine glasses and tumblers, and for bands of decoration round the bodies of decanters, carafes and sugar bowls. They remained in favour throughout the Victorian period and later, and are even used today. Other patterns consisted of floral ornament, such as stylised daisies and sprays of leaves, mostly patterns that could be executed in a series of continuous lines (Plates 78 and 85).

Much of the routine etching in Northwood's workshops was executed by women, either using one of the machines, or using an etching needle or stiletto to draw the patterns individually on the waxed surface of the glass. A tool called a 'dotter', made of boxwood and pointed at each end, was used to make dotted borders or details such as seeds or the centre of a flower. The etching needle or stiletto could only produce the etched lines of the pattern, with no shading or substance between the lines, and it was therefore necessary to obscure any solid parts of the etched pattern by using the engraver's wheel with a fine abrasive such as flour emery. This was a slow and tedious process. Northwood discovered a method of obscuring by means of acid, by neutralising the hydrofluoric acid with an alkali salt such as potassium carbonate or sodium carbonate. This compound attacked only the surface of the glass and did not eat into the glass. This partly neutralised acid became known as 'white acid' and was first used commercially in about 1867. It made the laborious obscuring by the engraver's wheel obsolete and the general effect was smoother, cleaner and more accurate in its application. The parts of the design that did not need obscuring were painted with an acid-resisting paint and the whole article was placed in the white acid for a time determined by the strength of the mixture. This process gave a great impetus to the development of etched designs, producing patterns that could more or less equal those of the more expensively produced engraved glass. White acid was also used for general obscuring purposes such as giving a satin finish to various fancy glasses.

More sophisticated and complicated methods of acid-etching were developed in the 1870s which involved transfer-printing from

81 Two-handled vase of clear glass with etched decoration by J. & J. Northwood, made by Stevens & Williams, Brierley Hill, to commemorate Queen Victoria's Jubilee of 1887. *Brierley Hill Collection.*

82 Vase of clear glass, template-etched by J. & J. Northwood, Stourbridge. Shown at the Paris Universal Exhibition of 1878. h. $8^1/_2$ in. *Borough of Stourbridge Collection.*

lithographic stones. Details of the process are given in a letter dated 1875 from H. G. Richardson to his son William Haden Richardson (1825–1913), who joined the firm of James Couper & Son, City Glass Works, Glasgow, in 1853. The resist for printing was itself a complicated substance, composed of two separate mixtures. The first consisted of almost equal quantities of juice pitch, pulverised and finely sifted, turpentine, and stearine, melted together. The second consisted of equal quantities of beeswax, resin, burgundy pitch and mutton suet. The final resist was achieved by melting the two together in the proportion of three and a half ounces of the first mixture to two and a half ounces of the second.

The desired pattern was painted on a flat, smooth lithographic stone with the resist. When dry, the edges of the pattern were enclosed with a ledge of wax to keep the acid on the pattern only when it was poured on to the stone. The acid used was one part muriatic acid to ten of water. The pattern was then worked over with a camel hair-brush and diluted acid until the stone was bitten into to the required depth for printing the impression. After this the acid was poured off, and the stone cleaned with turpentine. The resist was

83 Tumbler of clear glass with acid-etched decoration commemorating Queen Victoria's Diamond Jubilee of 1897. h. $4\frac{1}{4}$ in. *Private collection.*

put on to the stone, rubbed well into the pattern, the surplus being scraped off. A transfer paper was then placed on the stone which was put through the printing press. The printed pattern was then floated on water, pattern-side uppermost, ensuring that the upper surface did not get wet. The transfer print was then taken from the water and applied to the glass to be decorated, being rubbed well to press the pattern evenly over the surface. The paper was then soaked with muriatic acid and left for twelve hours. The paper was finally washed off, leaving the impression on the glass, which was placed in white acid to fix the pattern firmly.

This was evidently a slow and relatively costly process but the impressions of these printed acid-etched patterns in the Richardson pattern books of the late 1870s show that very fine effects could be achieved, almost equal to those produced by wheel-engraving. At Stevens & Williams, Frederick Carder used glass plates, about a quarter of an inch thick, for transfer etching as they were cheaper than metal or stone.

Transfer-printed etching was particularly suitable for pictorial patterns and was much used for souvenir and commemorative items. The tumbler illustrated in Plate 83 commemorating the Diamond Jubilee of 1897 is a fairly crude example. An elaborate series of commemorative items – tankards, jugs, vases, etc. – were produced by Richardson's in 1897, bearing the inscription 'In Commemoration of the Queen's Reign Longest Reign in History' and '18 Victoria 37' and '18 Victoria 97'. They also had medallion portraits of the Queen surmounted by a crown and encircled with a wreath of rose, thistle and shamrock. They were described as 'printed etched, rubbed in colour and gold'.

The Oriental influence that was manifest in most of the decorative arts in the 1880s was also apparent in the patterns of etched glass, being reflected in both Japanese and chinoiserie designs. A Richardson pattern book of 1888 shows a bottle etched with a design of Japanese warriors, copied more or less exactly from a Japanese woodcut, while other designs include six-sided bottles with Japanese-style birds and blossom in alternating panels. The traditional willow pattern was also used for etched decoration on claret jugs and glasses and also on glass plates.

Apart from its use for the cheaper or 'commercial' ranges of cameo glass, acid-etching was used to produce relief decoration on clear,

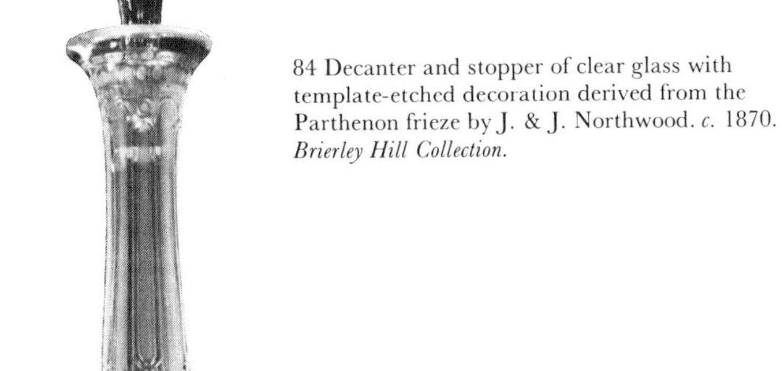

84 Decanter and stopper of clear glass with template-etched decoration derived from the Parthenon frieze by J. & J. Northwood. *c.* 1870. *Brierley Hill Collection.*

85 Decanter and stopper of clear glass with geometrical decoration. *c.* 1880. h. 12 in. *Victoria & Albert Museum.*

Glass Engraving

crystal glass. This was a relatively expensive process and was used chiefly for high-quality table glass as in the commemorative vase illustrated in Plate 81. This high-relief etched glass was generally advertised as 'carved' or 'sculptured' glass but it can be easily recognised by the hard, sharp edge to the motifs and the lack of graduation found in true carved glass.

A good deal of the surviving etched glass of the later nineteenth century is undoubtedly of foreign origin. Generally speaking, the etched decoration has a rougher, more scratched appearance than

86 Goblet of clear colourless glass with cut decoration and etched view of Balmoral Castle, commissioned for presents by Queen Victoria from John Ford, Holyrood Glass Works, Edinburgh. 1870–80. *Huntly House Museum, Edinburgh.*

on the best English examples. The foreign patterns, although elaborate, including many patterns incorporating rococo scrolls, are generally linear without any solid areas, and the decoration feels rough to the touch. The issue is somewhat complicated by the fact that a number of the Stourbridge firms in the late 1880s and 1890s imported foreign glass and etched it in their own workshops. The Richardson pattern books include a number of services of table glass which are marked 'Foreign' as well as a number of wine glasses designated as 'Foreign wines' which have geometric etched bands described as 'Temple Bros. etching'. Presumably these were to satisfy the cheaper end of Richardson's trade.

There is little doubt that the best of the English etched glass is among the most attractive productions of the Victorian period, producing patterns of great delicacy and refinement, although it has generally been considered inferior to engraved glass. This point was recognised in an article in the *Pottery Gazette* (2 January 1882). Having described the process of etching on glass, the author went on to describe its virtues as an art:

> The artist draws upon the glass the design as he would upon paper, he brings his inventive as well as his manipulative talent to bear upon his work and it is in every respect a drawing in itself, incapable of being reproduced except by applying the same labour – it is an art deserving encouragement and employs, or did employ, a great amount of labour produced by schools of design, by whom the early etched patterns were designed, and some of these have made their mark as artists in a much higher walk than decorating on glass. Etching should rank with engraving, and it is an absurd prejudice which displaces it; many designs are now produced by partly engraving and part etching and very pretty they are.

CHAPTER 8

VENETIAN-STYLE GLASS

A REVIVAL of interest in Venetian glass, and the special techniques associated with it, was manifest in England in the second half of the nineteenth century. The influence of this interest operated in several ways. It led not only to attempts to copy examples of old Venetian glass and revive past styles, but also to new types of glass that were essentially Victorian although their inspiration lay in the techniques and designs of the Venetian glass-makers of the fifteenth, sixteenth and seventeenth centuries. The Venetian influence was an important factor in the development of 'aesthetic' glass for an informed, intellectual taste, a taste that owed much to the theoretical writings of Ruskin, William Morris and Charles Lock Eastlake. Their formulations, the 'aesthetic' glass, and the glass of the Arts and Crafts movement is discussed in Chapter 10.

At a more popular level, the influence of Venetian glass led to a wide variety of fancy glass and novelties, much of which, in the finished products, appeared to have little to do with the original source of inspiration.

One of the first English glass manufacturers to take a serious interest in Venetian glass was Apsley Pellatt. In his *Curiosities of Glass Making*, published in London in 1849, Pellatt describes in considerable detail the processes of making the main types – Venetian filigree, *Mille-fiore*, Venetian Diamond Moulded, Venetian *Vitro di Trino*, and Old Venetian Frosted Glass. At the Great Exhibition of 1851, Pellatt showed in the catalogue of 'ice-glass' or 'craquelé' glass, which he described in the catalogue as 'Anglo-Venetian'. One of his pieces of 'ice-glass', a two-lipped wine-glass cooler, with an all-over

87 Water jug of 'ice-glass' with ribbed handle. *c.* 1885. h. 9$^{1}/_{8}$ in. *Private collection.*

cracked ice effect, was acquired by the Conservatoire National des Arts et Métiers, Paris. Other manufacturers quickly followed suit, and an ice-glass vase by Bacchus of Birmingham, with embedded fragments of coloured and opaline glass, decorated with bands of gilding, was acquired by the South Kensington Museum in 1853 (Plate 98). 'Ice-glass' was popular later too, particularly for water jugs as in the ribbed-handled example shown in Plate 87.

A Benjamin Richardson catalogue of about 1855–6 illustrates a service of 'Diamond Glass' described as 'blown by compressed Atmospheric Air by which a sharpness and brilliancy is obtained surpassing the best Examples of OLD VENETIAN GLASS from which it is copied'. The service, which included round-bellied long-necked decanters, water jugs and carafes, together with celery, wine glasses, tumblers, tankards, etc., does not, in the illustration, look at all Venetian, having the appearance of an all-over fine-cut diamond pattern. This appearance, however, is extremely close to that illustrated by Apsley Pellatt as 'Venetian Diamond Moulded' (Plate 101) in his *Curiosities of Glass Making*. Pellatt first describes the old Venetian method of blowing the glass into a projecting pillar-mould, the diamonds being formed by pinching the projecting pillars at equidistant points to form the diamond pattern. He goes on to say that 'Equally good effects are produced by modern glass makers in a more direct manner by making brass open and shut, or dip moulds, so as to give at one operation the entire diamond impression, thus saving the tedium of forming each diamond separately with the pucellas.' This was presumably the method used at Richardson's. The same Richardson catalogue illustrates a service described as 'Mediaeval Glass', which includes a water jug and claret jug with twisted rope handles, which appears to have a diamond air trap pattern (a process patented by Richardson in 1858) and which in fact looks more Venetian than the service purporting to be derived from Venetian models. Similar services appear in James Powell and Sons catalogue of the late 1850s, although they are described merely as moulded, and the word 'Venetian' does not appear (Plate 100). The catalogue also includes a Venetian-style chandelier, with rope twists, hanging bells and furnace-wrought twisted leaves, in clear, pink and turquoise glass, an example of which was purchased by the South Kensington Museum in 1866.

With few exceptions these early incursions into Venetian styles by

English manufacturers were not very close to the Venetian prototypes, although by the middle of the century not only manufacturers and designers but the public at large were able to see fine examples of old Venetian glass for themselves. In 1850, the Society of Arts mounted an exhibition of 'Ancient and Mediaeval Art', which included specimens of Venetian glass. In reviewing the exhibition, the *Art Journal* (1850 p. 102–103) remarked that 'In many of the Venetian glasses, salvers, vases, etc., the shapes are of the highest beauty and originality, and in some instances the application of colour is very peculiar'. Much of this glass was lent by Felix Slade (1790–1868). Slade, a Fellow of the Society of Arts, originally a collector of engravings and books relating to the fine arts, following several visits to Italy, turned his attention to Venetian glass. By the middle of the century he had formed a collection that was probably unrivalled, certainly at that time. He lent extensively from this collection of glass to many other exhibitions following that of 1850: to the Manchester Art Treasures Exhibition of 1857; an exhibition in the Ironmongers' Hall in 1861; a Loan Exhibition at the South Kensington Museum in 1862; and the Leeds Exhibition of 1868. On his death he bequeathed his glass collection, along with many other

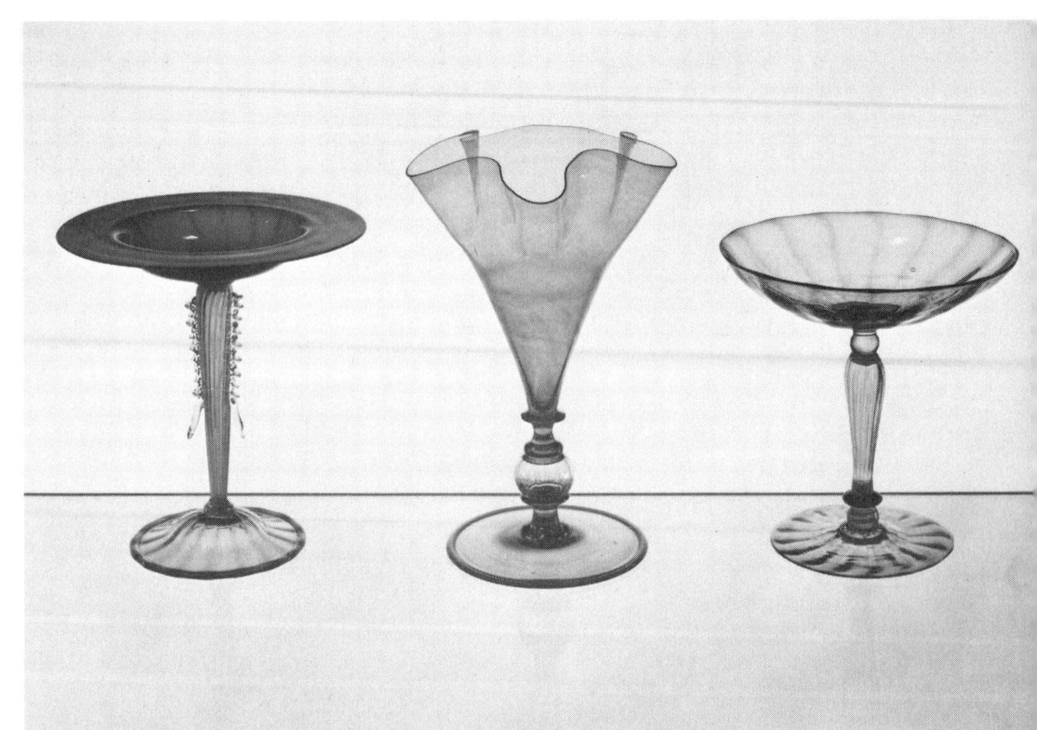

88 Three opalescent glasses in Venetian style made by James Powell & Sons, Whitefriars. 1876. h. $6^7/_8$ in., 9 in. and $6^3/_8$ in. *Victoria & Albert Museum.*

items, to the British Museum. Although it was put on view in 1868, the collection was not published until 1871 (*Catalogue of the Collection of Glass Formed by Felix Slade, Esq., F.S.A. with notes on the history of glass-making by Alexander Nesbit Esq., F.S.A.*) In Slade's own preface to the volume he states that 'The fragile products of the Venetian Glass Works attracted my attention many years since by their beauty and elegance of form. It was at a period when save for a few critical connoisseurs, they were but little cared for in England.' By the 1850s this was no longer the case and public bodies, such as the Department of Science and Art at South Kensington, and later at Edinburgh, began to build up extensive collections.

In 1853 the Museum of Ornamental Art (which was to become the South Kensington Museum in 1857 and later the Victoria & Albert Museum) acquired some thirty pieces of old Venetian glass. Further pieces were acquired throughout the 1850s, including some outstanding pieces from the Bernal Collection in 1855 and from the Soulages Collection in 1859. In 1858 the *Art Journal* devoted three articles to the collections of the South Kensington Museum, describing objects which it considered would provide suitable inspiration for designers and manufacturers, singling out the Venetian glass as

89 Goblet and jug of opalescent glass with a standing bowl of green glass with clear glass handles made in the Venetian style by James Powell & Sons, Whitefriars. 1876. h. 8 5/8 in., 4 1/2 in. and 7 in. *Victoria & Albert Museum.*

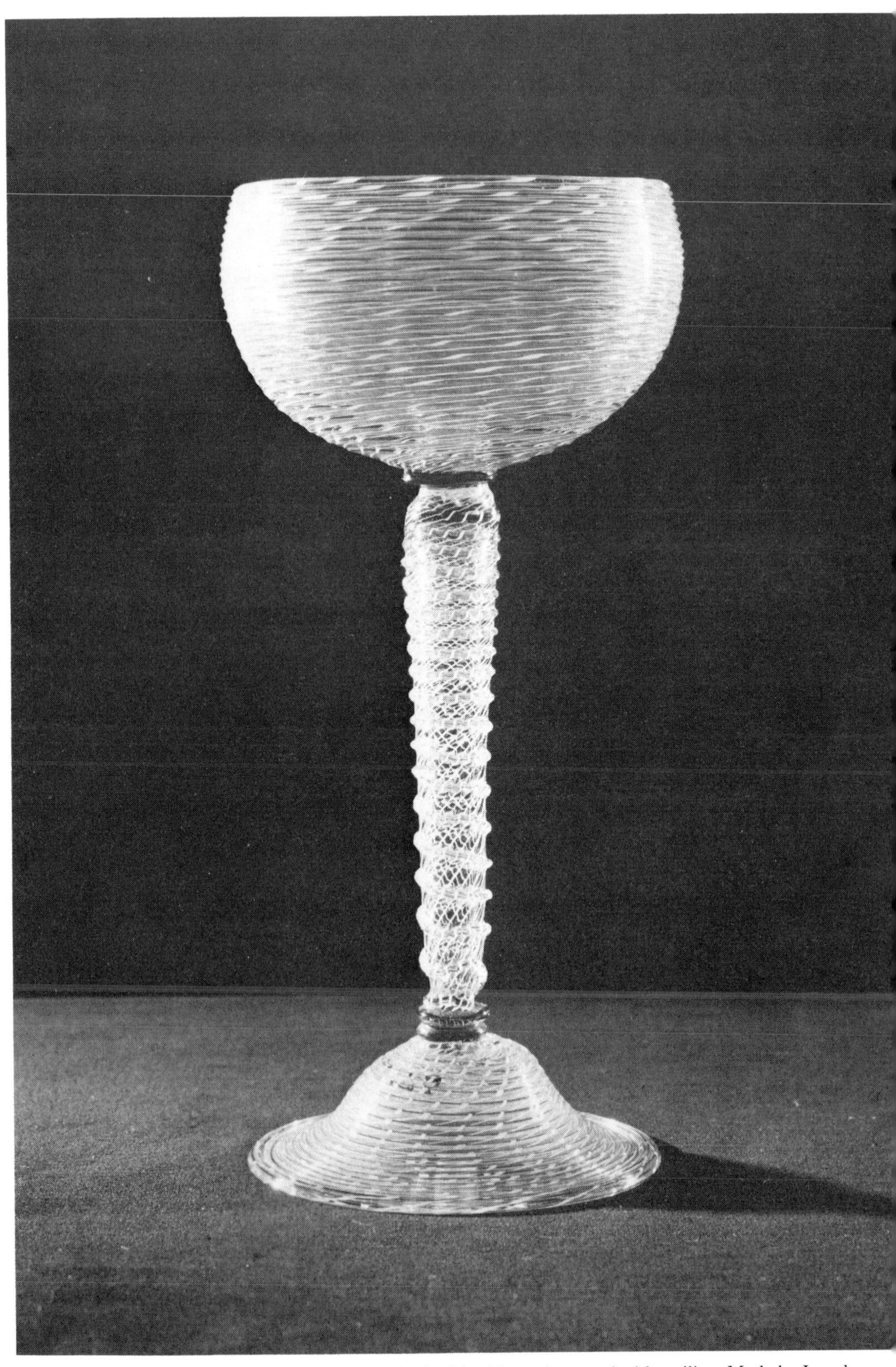

90 Goblet of blue-green glass striped with white and covered with trailing. Made by Joseph Leicester at James Powell & Sons, Whitefriars, and awarded a Society of Arts prize for 1869 to 1870. h. $8^1/_2$ in. *Victoria & Albert Museum.*

being chosen 'for simple elegance of form . . . the varieties being almost infinite'.

This interest in old Venetian glass coincided with a revival of the glass industry in Venice and Murano, which had suffered a decline in the eighteenth century. In 1835 there was a revival of the old processes of glass-working in Venice, commenced by Sig. D. Bupolin, and followed by Cav. Petro Bigaglia and Lorenzo Radi. This revival did not escape the notice of the authorities in South Kensington and in 1860 the Museum acquired a group of modern *calcedonio* glasses by Lorenzo Radi. From then on modern Venetian glass continued to be bought alongside earlier specimens. In the 1860s the leading figure in the Venetian revival was undoubtedly Dr Antonio Salviati, whose glass was first seen in London at the 1862 International Exhibition. The South Kensington Museum made its first purchases of Venetian glass from Salviati in 1863, when it acquired two elaborate chandeliers and two candelabra.

Dr Antonio Salviati was originally an *avvocato* in Venice but he gave up this profession for the study of the art of the Middle Ages, particularly mosaics and glass. He became associated with Lorenzo Radi and others and set up his company at Murano for the manufacture of mosaics and glassware about 1859. From the onset he received a good deal of encouragement from English sources, notably from Sir Austen Henry Layard, the prominent English politician and excavator of Nineveh. This led to the formation of an English company, with Dr Salviati as the Artistic Director and Layard as its chief promoter. Sir William Drake, author of a volume on *Venetian Ceramics* and Sir William Tite were also Directors. A catalogue, illustrated in colour, with the prices in English currency, entitled *Salviati & Company Ltd.*, *Venetian Gallery* with addresses at 731 Campo San Vio, Venice, and 431 Oxford Street, London, is prefaced by an article from *The Times* (19 October 1866), headed 'The Glass Workers of Murano' in which it is stated that an Anglo-Italian Company was about to be formed by Salviati. The *Art Journal* catalogue of the Paris Exhibition of 1867, at which Salviati showed a considerable quantity of Venetian glass, described him as being 'of Venice, and now also of London.' The next year, in 1868, showrooms were established at 30 St James's Street, and the company eventually became known as the Venice and Murano Glass Company Limited.

FLINT, OR PALE GREEN GLASS. } PLAIN, RIBBED, OR DIAMOND MOULDED.

1/3 FULL SIZE.

JAMES POWELL & SONS
WHITEFRIARS GLASS WORKS,
TEMPLE St E.C.

Maclure & Macdonald, Lithrs to the Queen.

The *Art Journal* of 1866 (p. 257) described Salviati's imitations of the old Venetian glass as 'the most successful we have yet seen . . . all these pieces are so close an imitation that it behoves collectors of ancient glass to be on their guard, for it is difficult for any but the most expert judges to discriminate between the old and the new'. As was to be expected, Salviati's Venetian glass appealed mainly to a fairly sophisticated antiquarian taste and to those who wanted something different from the ordinary flint glass decorated by cutting and engraving.

Charles Lock Eastlake, however, who was as vehement as Ruskin and Morris in condemning the modern styles of cut glass (see Chapter 10), was enthusiastic in his praise of Salviati. In his *Hints on Household Taste* (London, 1868) he describes how Salviati, 'encouraged by the advice of some English artist friends', re-established at Venice a manufactory of table glass 'which, in quality of material, excellence of design, and spirit of workmanship, soon promised to rival anything of the kind which had been produced. Indeed there seems little reason why it should fall short of former excellence. . . Dr Salviati did his best to procure good designs and old examples for

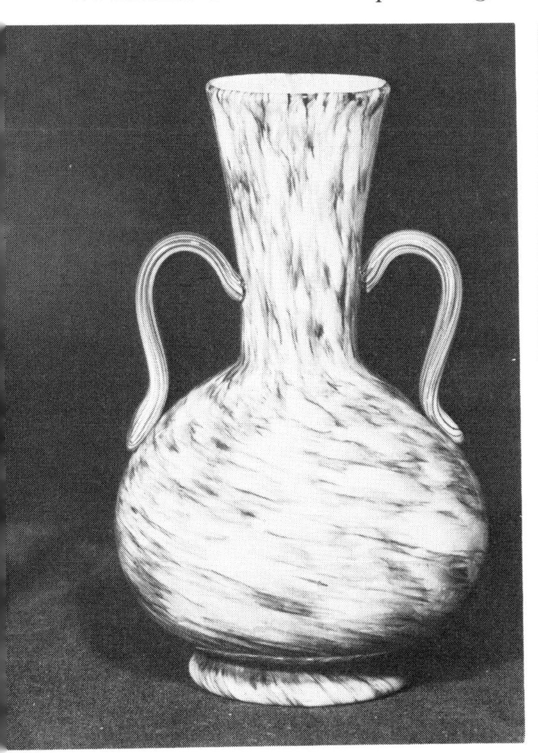

91 Vase in Venetian style mottled in blue and white and flecked with crimson. Alexander D. Jenkinson, Norton Park Glass Works, Edinburgh. *c.* 1880. h. 7 in. *Royal Scottish Museum, Edinburgh.*

92 Vase in Venetian style of deep amber-coloured glass spirally flecked in white. Alexander D. Jenkinson, Norton Park Glass Works. *c.* 1880. h. 6$^{1}/_{8}$ in. *Royal Scottish Museum, Edinburgh.*

93 Jug and tumbler in clear glass with opaque white latticinio decoration. Alexander D. Jenkinson, Norton Park Glass Works. *c.* 1880. h. $5^1/_4$ in. and $3^1/_4$ in. *Royal Scottish Museum, Edinburgh.*

his men to copy'. Eastlake devotes several pages and a complete sheet of illustrations to Salviati's glass, which included water bottles, claret jugs, tumblers, wine and liqueur glasses, salt-cellars, preserves, flower stands, tazzas and vases – indeed, every conceivable kind of table and ornamental glass. Many of the goblets were decorated with flowers and pinched ornaments below the bowl, others had a stem formed by a snake or serpent. Air trap decoration, called by Eastlake 'bubble filigree' was much used, a type of decoration that was to be much used by English manufacturers in the satin glass of the 1880s. Another revival of Salviati's that was to be widely imitated by English firms was what Eastlake described as the old Dutch type of water-bottle, which:

> with its round capacious bowl of thin glass strengthened at intervals with little twisted ribs of the same material, was manufactured in Venice also, and frequently decorated with colour. It is

I Carafe, clear flint glass with painted decoration, the base marked 'RICHARDSON'S VITRIFIED' in red. Made by W. H., B. & J. Richardson, Stourbridge. *c.* 1850. h. $9^1/_2$ in.
Private collection.

II Jug and basket of blue 'Pearline' glass made by George Davidson, Teams Glass Works, Gateshead. The jug is marked with a serial registration mark for 1 August 1894 and the basket is illustrated in the *Pottery Gazette* supplement of 1 July 1891. Jug h. 7 in. Basket h. $3^1/_2$ in. *Private collection.*

III Three examples of pressed glass: *Left* Swan vase made by Sowerby & Co. Although this example is unmarked a vase of this design was bought by the Museum of Decorative Arts in Prague direct from Sowerby & Co. in 1868. h. 7 in. *Centre* Dessert plate in jet (dark purple) glass made by Henry Greener, Sunderland, and registered 29 July 1876. diam. $8^3/_4$ in. *Right* Miniature boat in opalescent glass made by Burtles, Tate & Co., Manchester. Marked with serial registration number for 1885. l. $7^1/_4$ in. *Private collection*.

IV Decanter and stopper of clear, colourless glass with etched decoration in 'Alhambresque' style, with applied ruby and emerald glass 'jewels' and gilding. Made by Apsley Pellatt & Company, Falcon Glass Works, London. 1862. Part of a service of the same design was exhibited at the London International Exhibition of 1862. h. $10^1/_2$ in. *Victoria & Albert Museum.*

V Vase of silvered glass cut on the wheel through a blue glass overlay. Marked on base 'H. THOMSON LONDON PATENT'. Probably made by James Powell & Sons, London. *c.* 1850. h. 8 in. *Victoria & Albert Museum.*

VI Three-colour cameo glass vase made by Thomas Webb, Stourbridge. *c.* 1890. Possibly executed by J. T. Fereday. h. $9^1/_2$ in. *Sotheby's Belgravia*.

VII 'The Milton Vase'. Cameo glass with scenes of the expulsion of Adam and Eve from the Garden of Eden, this view showing the angel Gabriel. Commissioned by Philip Pargeter from John Northwood and exhibited at the Paris Exhibition of 1878. Signed and dated 'John Northwood 1878'. h. $13^{3}/_{8}$ in. *Sotheby's Belgravia*.

VIII Centrepiece or flower stand of opalescent glass with furnace-wrought decoration. English, probably Stourbridge. *c.* 1895–1900. h. 22 in. *Sotheby's Belgravia.*

now produced at the price of a common wine decanter. In like manner the sturdy green hock glasses which were once imported from Holland have been imitated and improved by Salviati, for whereas their broad ribbed stem was not infrequently cast or blown into a mould those just sent over from Venice have stems composed of an actual cord of glass wound spirally round, and so spreading outwards to form a foot.

While Salviati's glass was much praised in the art magazines of the time, it did not escape criticism from some quarters, attracting the same kind of denunciation that some of Morris & Company's exhibits elicited at the 1862 London Exhibition, a criticism engendered by the very success in imitating ancient styles. A Mr T. J. Wilkinson, a practical glass-worker from Birmingham, in his report to the Society of Arts on the Paris Exhibition of 1876, states that:

> the greatest display [in the Italian section] is made by Dr Salviati of Venice . . . the works displayed here are as odd-looking and as grotesque in their appearance as we should consider any number of men who thought fit to dress themselves in the habiliments of the Middle Ages; that being the era the glass is supposed to be a copy of. All very well to put in the studio, or on the sideboards of the wealthy, but for aught else it is entirely useless.

Dr Salviati did, however, make a few excursions from historic forms, especially for the English market, when he entered into an arrangement with M. E. Rimmel, the perfumer – described by the *Art Journal* for 1866 as 'a man of taste, and a veritable artist in his peculiar profession of providing elegancies for the toilette and boudoir'. For Rimmel, Salviati produced centrepieces for the table and fountains for dispensing rosewater and other essences, which, while enriched with Venetian-style ornaments, could be made to a variety of designs. Specimens could be seen at Rimmel's showrooms at 128 Regent Street and at 96 The Strand. These productions of Rimmel and Salviati no doubt contributed to the development of the typical Victorian centrepieces described in Chapter 9.

By the time Salviati had established himself in London, a number of British firms were successfully producing Venetian-style glass, including James Powell & Sons who exhibited glass in the Venetian style at the Paris Exhibition of 1867. An outstanding group of Powell's Venetian glass was acquired by the South Kensington

94 Dish of clear glass with opaque white latticinio decoration. Alexander D. Jenkinson, Norton Park Glass Works. *c.* 1880. diam $10^3/_8$ in. *Royal Scottish Museum, Edinburgh.*

Museum in 1876. It includes standing bowls and tazzas in pale green glass, some with furnace-wrought handles and decorations in clear glass; dark green glass with pulled *latticinio* decoration and spiral threading in blue glass, and particularly attractive opalescent glass shading from milky white to a deep turquoise blue (Plates 88, 89 and 102). This opalescent glass was used not only for wine glasses, finger bowls, etc., but also for tall, trumpet-shaped vases with waved tops, some with diamond moulded patterns, glass that anticipated the almost art nouveau glass of the turn of the century. A particularly sophisticated example of Powell's Venetian glass is the goblet by Joseph Leicester shown in Plate 90. The goblet, of blue-green glass

95 Vase in Venetian style of brown glass mottled and streaked in grey, red and white with applied furnace-wrought decoration. Alexander D. Jenkinson, Norton Park Glass Works. *c.* 1880. h. 7 in. *Royal Scottish Museum, Edinburgh.*

96 Vase in Venetian style in mottled blue, green and white glass. Alexander D. Jenkinson, Norton Park Glass Works. *c.* h. 5½ in. *Royal Scottish Museum, Edinburgh.*

striped with white and covered with trailing received a prize at the Society of Arts Competition of 1869–70. Joseph Leicester, the son of a Warrington glass-blower, was born in 1825. He worked as a glass-blower from the age of ten, for many years at James Powell & Sons. He then became secretary of the Glass Blowers' Friendly Society and a prominent temperance advocate, with radical views. In 1885 he was elected, on a Liberal/Labour ticket, as Member of Parliament for the newly formed constituency of West Ham South but lost his seat in the General Election in the following year. In 1892 he was adopted as Liberal candidate for West Ham South but withdrew on the eve of the election in favour of Keir Hardie, in the interests of radical unity. It is a strange irony that so strong an advocate of temperance should spend most of his life producing vessels for the consumption of alcoholic liquor.

97 Covered bowl and covered vase with ribbed decoration and opaque blue drops on the vase. Made by Isaac Barnes, Birmingham. *c.* 1870–5. h. 7½ in. and 9½ in. *City Museum and Art Gallery, Birmingham.*

Powell's again exhibited Venetian-style glass at the Paris Exhibition of 1878, glass that was described by the *Saturday Review* and other periodicals as the finest in the building. The fact that Joseph Leicester worked for Powell's did not inhibit him in praising their products in his review of the exhibition for the Society of Arts (*The Society of Arts Artisan Reports at the Paris Universal Exhibition of 1878*):

> This firm has admirably shown in the character of its work how beautiful glass can be made in the most artistic way with great economy of human labour. Sir Charles Eastlake and Mr Ruskin would have been in raptures at this realisation of their ideas. Light as Venetian, pure as the diamond and diverging from all the paths trodden by other manufacturers, this exhibit well illustrated utility with beauty of form and colour. It taught in the plainest

98 Vase of 'ice-glass', with imbedded fragments of coloured and opaline glass and gilt band. Made by George Bacchus & Sons, Birmingham. *c.* 1853. h. $7^{1}/_{4}$ in. *Victoria & Albert Museum.*

> characters that ornamentation should only be of the subjective kind; that the material, glass, can radiate a lustre richer than any the jugglery of iron and stone wheels can confer, and that the substance itself should be formed so as to reflect its own beautiful and imperishable gleam. This was the leading idea of those old Venetians who did such wonders with glass in the days of old, and it has been caught, wrought out, developed and modernised to perfection in this group of articles.

After describing the glass in some detail, which followed the same styles as that purchased by the South Kensington Museum in 1877, he concludes by stating that 'the opal in which they abound is certainly superior to anything even in the Venetian court'.

Another of the leading firms in the production of Venetian-style glass in the 1870s was Alexander D. Jenkinson of the Leith Walk Glass Works, Edinburgh. The works were erected in 1864 by a glass manufacturer called J. Thomas and sold to Alexander Jenkinson the following year. In 1876 the premises were extended at Norton Park and in 1919 they were acquired by Webb's Crystal Glass Company.

In an article in the *Art Journal* (1875 p. 365), 'On the Progress of Our Art Industries', Professor Archer, the Director of the Museum of Science and Art at Edinburgh (now the Royal Scottish Museum), emphasises the success of Alexander Jenkinson in the imitation of Venetian glass:

> Some of the operatives possess such remarkable skill and intelligence that, were it not for the constant demand upon their time in the production of their staple articles of manufacture, they would certainly produce much of novelty and excellence. They work in *reticella*, in moulding and pinching, in jewelling and floral ornamentation, and indeed in nearly all the processes of the Venetian glass workers, with such skill that it is not too much to hope that the time is not far distant when, if not rivals, they will be no mean competitors with their brother workmen in Murano.

There follows the implied criticism that the exquisite purity of the material – 'water itself is not more clear or transparent' – which entailed a certain weight, precluded the hope of attaining the almost aeriel lightness, combined with strength, which made Venetian glass unique. Their success, however, was attributed by Professor Archer largely to the fact that the Edinburgh glass-workers made full use of

99 Vase of clear colourless glass with applied ribbed shells and raspberry prunts in deep opaque turquoise-blue glass. Birmingham or Stourbridge. *c.* 1870. *Private collection.*

100 Decanter and stopper in clear colourless glass, the body mould-blown in Venetian diamond pattern, the neck cut in broad flutes. Made by James Powell & Sons, Whitefriars. *c.* 1855. *Private collection.*

the facilities for study offered by the fine collection of ancient and modern glass built up by the Edinburgh Museum of Science and Art, a collection which included a superb display of old Venetian glass formed by the Abbate Zannetti, Director of the Museum at Murano. Professor Archer ends his article by recording 'that the Saturday half-holiday is looked upon as a much prized means of studying these examples by the better class of workman in Scotland'. It has been said (although I can find no firm evidence to support it) that Italian glass-makers were employed by Jenkinson, but whether this is true or no, there is little doubt that their *latticinio* glassware in particular (see Plates 93, 94) was a very creditable imitation of the Venetian prototypes. The firm also produced 'Schmeltz' or semi-opaque mottled glass, usually in the form of vases with applied handles made of canes of coloured glass, which were derived from Venetian prototypes (Plates 91, 92, 95 and 96).

Indeed like Salviati's, some of Jenkinson's Venetian-style glass was criticised because it was so manifestly imitative. Joseph Leicester, whose review of Powell's glass at the Paris Exhibition of 1878 for the Society of Arts has already been quoted, was less enthusiastic in describing the exhibits of Alexander Jenkinson: 'Here is marvellous work, showing qualities of manipulation, capable of accomplishing anything worthy of being done; yet nearly all these products are imitations. . . . If imitation may be taken to imply flattery, then assuredly the Venetians are flattered by this firm. . . . One gets tired of the constant repetition of a Venetian goblet, a Venetian vase, a Venetian jug, as if nothing else in the world could be made. . . . Let us hope that this firm will yet find out a purer field of activity than the Venetian'.

Somewhat similar to some of Powell's Venetian-style glass was the Venetian Glass of Sowerby & Company's Ellison Glass Works, Newcastle upon Tyne, although it was cruder and less thinly blown. This glass appears to have been made in the late 1860s and 1870s, and consisted of jugs, footed tumblers and vases, made in olive green glass, with pale blue rims, sometimes decorated with blue threads and applied prunts. Some of the jugs had round bellies with short necks, others were taller with ovoid bodies and the shapes were deliberately slightly irregular. It was also made in clear glass, again with pale blue rims. Although the inspiration was said to be Venetian, it possibly has more affinity with the Nailsea and Bristol glass of the early nineteenth century.

101 Claret jug of clear colourless glass, the lower portion mould-blown in Venetian diamond pattern, the upper portion and handle wheel-engraved. Made by Apsley Pellatt & Co., Falcon Glass Works. *Sotheby's Belgravia.*

Apart from glass which sought to imitate Venetian glass in general shape and style, the Venetian influence was also apparent in various isolated features on more typical styles of English Victorian crystal glass. A fashion for the ribbing of components, often referred to as 'shell' decoration, was characteristic of the 1870s and 1880s. A ribbed handle was first registered by Thomas Webb's in 1867, which was quickly imitated by other firms, and was much used for the handles of water jugs, celery vases, etc. Applied ribbed 'shell' ornaments and feet were used to decorate vases, and are found on all types of fancy glass. The applied prunts or 'raspberries', various 'jewelled' effects, rope twists for handles and centrepieces, furnace wrought leaves, pincerings, etc., all owed their introduction to the Venetian influence (Plates 97, 99). These manifestations are described in more detail in the chapters on 'Centrepieces and Flower Stands', and 'Later Fancy Glass'. Similarly, the fashion for waved and crimped rims, manifest on flower stands and vases from 1870 onwards, derives ultimately from Venetian sources. The streaked and marbled effects and the use of aventurine, as well as the more general use of colour in fancy glass, also arose from the Venetian

102 Vase and jug of opalescent glass with threads of blue glass, made by James Powell & Sons, Whitefriars. 1876. *Victoria & Albert Museum.*

influence, an influence that by the 1880s, certainly as far as fancy glass at a popular level was concerned, had become so diffuse and dissipated as to be hardly recognisable.

The more conscious expression of the Venetian influence, as evinced particularly in the glass of James Powell & Sons, was essentially part of the 'aesthetic' movement, leading to the Arts and Crafts movement, producing glass that appealed to an informed, somewhat intellectual taste.

CHAPTER 9

CENTREPIECES AND FLOWER STANDS

ONE of the most original developments in the latter half of the nineteenth century was the evolution of elaborate, composite glass centrepieces, intended primarily for the display of flowers. Various epergnes and centrepieces, combining candelabra with cut-glass bon bon dishes had been fashionable since the eighteenth century but the type of centrepiece that developed in the 1860s and 1870s owed little to past styles. Their evolution can be charted fairly accurately through the records of the Patent Office Design Registry, by the extant pattern books of a number of the Stourbridge firms and by illustrations in contemporary periodicals.

It will be seen, however, that the development was extremely complex, as a new feature, pioneered by one firm, would be taken over and combined with an idea introduced by another, in a gradual process of evolution, culminating in the mid-1870s in the typical Victorian flower stand consisting of a central trumpet-shaped vase surrounded by a symmetrical arrangement of subsidiary flower holders. The whole was usually mounted on a crimped bowl, for holding fruit or flowers, or on a circular base or *plateau* of mirrored glass. This type of centrepiece continued in production until the early 1920s, and undoubtedly many of the extant specimens, purporting to be Victorian, are of a considerably later date.

The starting-point was a single trumpet-shaped flower vase springing from the centre of a standing bowl with a high or low foot. These simple flower stands, originating about the middle of the century continued in production throughout the Victorian era and were an integral part of the normal complete table service being decorated with engraving or etching according to the prevalent fashion. The first registrations for composite flower stands were made by the London dealers, Dobson & Pearce in June 1861. The basic design consisted of a central trumpet-shaped vase set on a twisted circlet (which looked like a glass rope) with a knop below, decorated with 'raspberry' prunts, on a spreading foot in the shape of an inverted bell. In one case two, in the other, four, side vases were supported by smaller twisted circlets. These were almost certainly designed by Daniel Pearce, a partner in the firm, who was a few years later, in 1867, described by the *Art Journal*, as 'unrivalled in England as a designer of works in glass'. By this time Daniel Pearce had moved to the firm of W. P. & G. Phillips, and later, in the 1870s, he joined Thomas Webb, where he continued to specialise in flower stands and centrepieces. These new flower stands by Dobson & Pearce were an outstanding feature at the London International Exhibition of 1862 and a similar flower stand was shown by James Powell & Sons (illustrated on Plate 116 of J. B. Waring, *Masterpieces of Industrial Art and Sculpture at the International Exhibition of 1862*

103 Group of glass, including two flower stands, exhibited by James Powell & Sons, Whitefriars, at the London International Exhibition of 1862. Plate from J. B. Waring's *Masterpieces of Industrial Art from the London International Exhibition of 1862.*

(London, 1862) (Plate 103). Various further combinations of fixed trumpet vases with rope twists were registered by Dobson & Pearce between 1862 and 1864, and a further development, initiated by another London dealer, Naylor & Company, was a substitution of the subsidiary trumpet vases by 'cornucopiae'. By this time, not only the London dealers, but the Stourbridge firms of Boulton & Mills and Hodgetts, Richardson & Pargeter, were registering similar designs. The catalogue of John Ford of the Holyrood Glass Works, Edinburgh, dating from the late 1860s, also includes a 'cornucopia' flower stand with a bowl with three ball feet at the base and a tall double-twist stem supporting a smaller bowl with three fixed cornucopiae and a central trumpet vase. A similar flower stand also appears in a James Powell & Sons' catalogue of approximately the same date. Innumerable variants on this theme occur throughout the 1860s and the classical or Roman influence, seen in the cornucopiae, was often enhanced by the use of applied lion masks and by hanging chains or festoons of glass drops.

Many examples of this type of flower stand are found in a pattern book issued by Philip Pargeter, Red House Glass Works, Stourbridge, which describes him as a 'Manufacturer of Registered Flower Centres, Candelabra, Vases, Specimen Tubes, and of Cut, Engraved and Etched Glass'. The first design in the book, an elaborate flower stand with hanging baskets and applied leaves (a type that will be fully described later) was registered in August 1871, the year Pargeter set up on his own as a glass manufacturer, but a number of the designs are undoubtedly of an earlier date. Some of them are identical to the flower stands which appear in a book of photographs of Richardson's glass dated 1867. Philip Pargeter served his apprenticeship under his uncle, W. B. Richardson, working there as an engraver until 1852. He then set up an engraving shop of his own but in 1863 returned to his old firm, setting up in partnership with W. B. Richardson and J. W. Hodgetts, the firm then becoming Hodgetts, Richardson & Pargeter. In 1871 he again set up on his own at the Red House Glass Works, Stourbridge, where he remained until he sold the business to Stuart & Sons in 1882.

Another stage in the development of composite flower stands was the incorporation of hanging baskets, an idea that had been introduced by James Powell & Sons at the 1862 International Exhibition in an elaborate centrepiece which combined candelabrum and flower stand. The first registration of hanging baskets as part of a flower stand was made by the London dealer James Green in March 1866. The baskets were arranged round the central vase, suspended from curved supports which sprang from a socket block placed immediately above the supporting bowl. Similar registrations by Hodgetts, Richardson & Pargeter followed later in the year and in 1867 George Wallis's review of the Paris Exhibition of 1867 in the *Art Journal Catalogue* remarks that 'the variety of these flower stands is very great, and gives evidence of great demand'. Indeed, by this time the flower stand had already become something in the nature of a status symbol and an essential embellishment of the fashionable dinner table.

The next stage in the development came in the early 1870s, when mirror bases or plateaux were used as a substitute for the bowl, and additional decorations in the form of Venetian-inspired glass 'fern leaves' were introduced (Plate 105). The first registration of a mirror base, which was intended to reflect the flowers as in a pool of water, was by the Stourbridge firm of Boulton & Mills on 25 January 1871, in which baskets like bell-shaped flowers were suspended from curved supports, like barley sugar twists, around a central vase with a crimped top. The first registration incorporating fern leaves was made by Philip Pargeter in 1873, in a design that also included hanging baskets and a mirror base. By this time the use of crimping round the top of the central vase, hanging baskets and supporting bowl was almost universal. The introduction of colour, used only sparingly in the mid-1860s, became more common. The earlier flower stands were nearly always in clear crystal glass and, although elaborate, were formal in appearance, but as the century advanced the flower stands became plant-like in appearance and often as colourful as the flowers they held.

The botanical influence is also seen in the introduction of bulrushes, often in obscured or threaded glass, as an alternative to the fern leaves. Several instances of this occur in Stevens & Williams' record books in 1875 and the centrepiece illustrated in Plate 104, probably of Stourbridge manufacture, is a typical example.

By the mid-1870s the most popular type of Victorian centrepiece, with a crimped trumpet-shaped central vase with matching subsidiary vases or hanging baskets, was firmly established, being modified only by minor changes in shape or added decorative features, and by

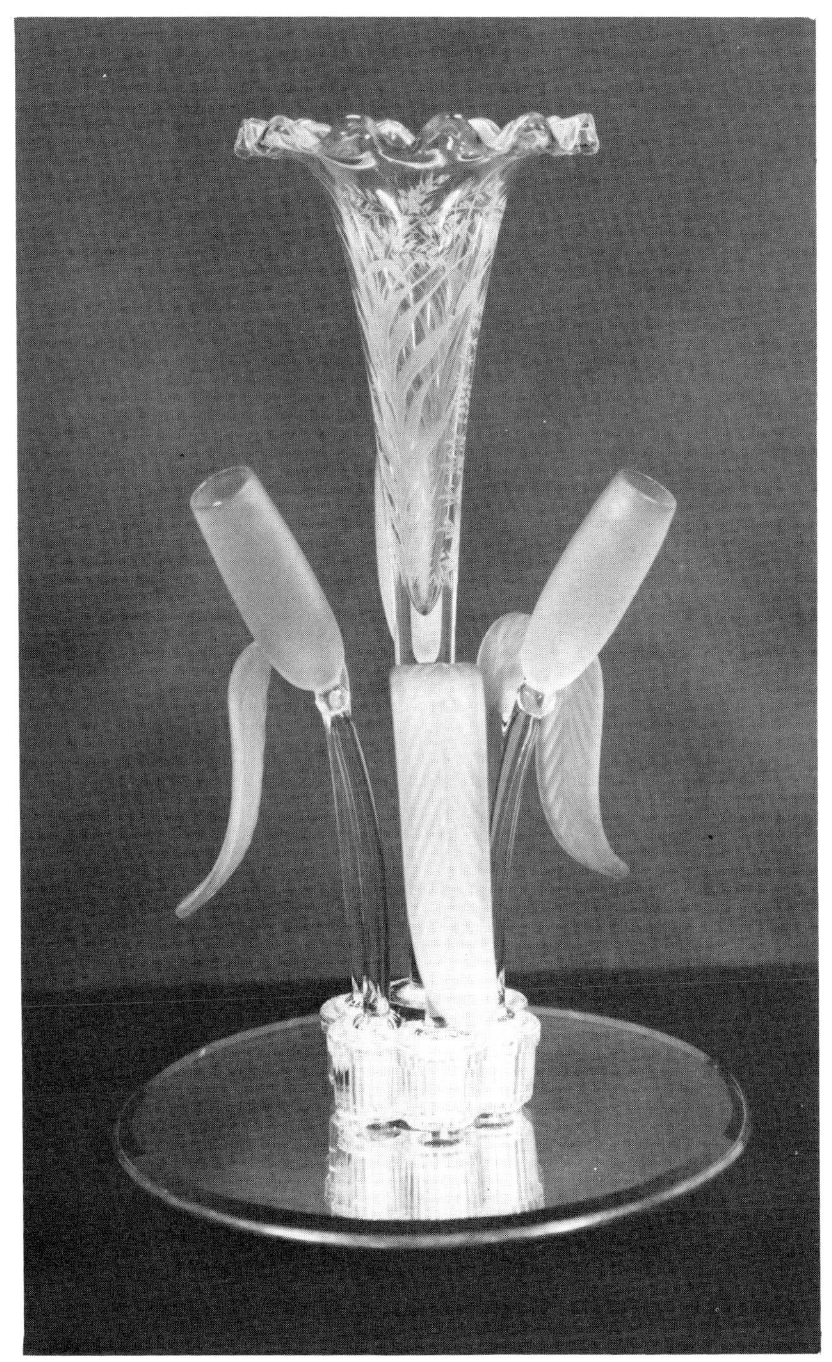

104 Flower stand with engraved decoration and 'bulrushes' on a mirror plateau. Probably Stourbridge. *c.* 1875. *Victoria & Albert Museum.*

the increasing use of colour. A significant development that seemed to occur in the 1880s, and is a marked feature of the later flower stands, was the raising of the centre of the supporting bowl into a steep cone, so that the socket block was placed well above the rim (Plate 106).

The centrepieces that were made in clear crystal glass were often decorated by engraving, particularly in fern designs, or with bands of threading at the top of the vases, often in a contrasting colour, such as pale blue. Increasingly throughout the 1880s coloured glass of all shades was employed – ruby, blue and amber – and many shades of tinted opalescent ranging through citron, pink and, above all, turquoise. The vases and baskets were often decorated with spiral trails in clear or coloured glass and with applied 'frills' of crimped ornament. 'Seaweed' and 'coral' decorations were also applied. Less frequently such flower stands were made with 'pull-up' decoration or in ivory glass with decoration in gold and silver.

This type of composite flower stand remained in production until about 1923 (many illustrations can be found in the *Pottery Gazette* in the early 1920s) and filtered down to the most popular level, being found in urban working-class homes and country cottages, the cheaper and cruder examples being made in the backyard 'cribs'. Alongside these, other types of flower stands and table decorations were introduced throughout the 1880s and 1890s.

A much squatter and somewhat more robust type of flower stand, introduced about 1880, consisted of a circular mirror plateau (often set on a velvet-covered base) with a central vase and three matching vases or baskets set close to the plateau, usually on plain stems of clear glass. The vases or baskets were often globular in form, closely resembling gas moons, or sometimes bucket-, melon- or tulip-shaped. If made in crystal glass they were usually decorated with engraved or etched designs of flowers, leaves and ferns. Shell-like vases, a type registered by John Walsh Walsh in 1885 as their 'New Conchoidal Glass', were also employed. A flower stand by John Walsh Walsh of this type is described by the *Pottery Gazette* (February 1885 p. 179), as 'an epergne with opaque scallop shells of a pinkish tint to hold fruit or sweets, mounted on a mirror in the shape of a grape leaf'. Other shells, more horn-like in form, were made in threaded glass. Coinciding with the general revival of cut glass in the later 1880s, many had vases in richly cut glass, sometimes in the form of a thistle or an acorn. Such flower stands seem to have been a

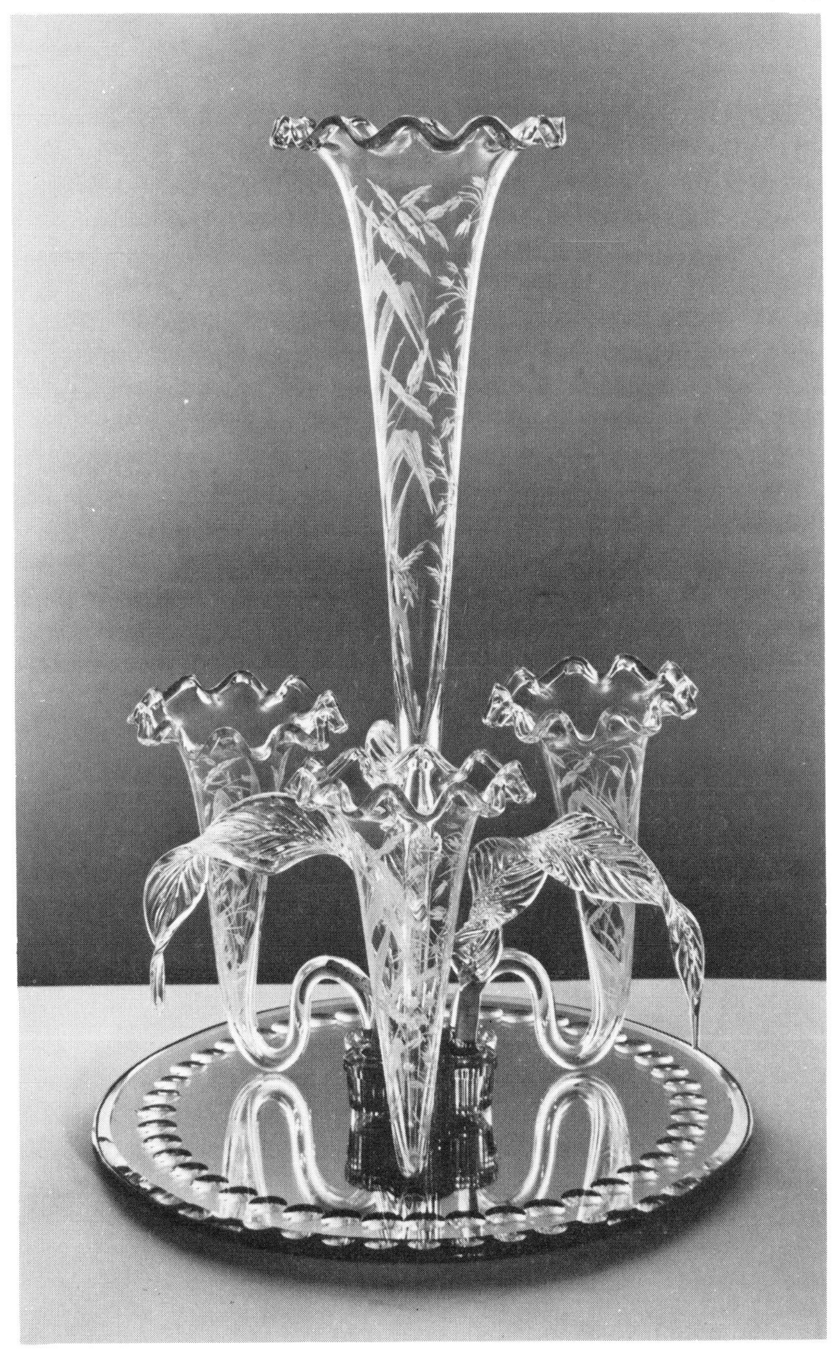

105 Flower stand in clear colourless glass with engraved decoration on the vases and furnace-wrought leaves, with a mirror plateau. Probably Stourbridge. *c.*1875. *Victoria & Albert Museum.*

speciality of H. G. Richardson & Sons, who also made elaborate examples cased in ruby and richly cut. Fairy lights were also incorporated into these flower stands, and examples were made by Stevens & Williams in their registered 'Matsu-no-kee' glass. A catalogue of Smart Brothers, Round Oak Glass Works, Brierley Hill, dating from the later 1880s, illustrates many of these flower stands with engraved and etched vases, and others in ruby glass decorated with applied acanthus leaves in crystal. A similar example by Burtles & Tate, Manchester, is illustrated in the *Pottery Gazette* (14 October 1884). The catalogues of Silber & Fleming, wholesalers and importers, dating from 1882 to 1889, provide numerous illustrations of every type of flower stand and give a clear indication of the wide variety available (Plates 107 and 108). It is not often possible to attribute these to a particular manufacturer; indeed, some of them are probably of foreign origin.

The naturalism seen in the foregoing types of flower stands, was further developed from 1885 onwards. The Silber & Fleming catalogue of 1885 includes table decorations consisting of a single vase in pink opalescent glass, shaped like a large inverted bell flower, or a tulip, with calyx and large floppy leaves in green glass, the whole being mounted on a circular mirror plateau with a scalloped edge.

Flower tubes formed as a rustic tree-trunk, either singly or in groups, were produced by the firm of John Walsh Walsh of Birmingham and by a number of the Stourbridge firms from 1885 onwards. Similar rustic tree-trunks were made by George Davidson of Gateshead in their registered 'Pearline' glass. Other similar flower tubes were made to imitate cactus stems. Both the rustic tree-trunks and cactus stems were used to support baskets in an asymetrical arrangement. John Walsh Walsh of Birmingham produced an endless variety of cactus flower stands which were described by the *Pottery Gazette* (August 1889) as 'a beautiful ornament even without flowers'. Similar cactus flower stands and vases, in ruby and flint glass, were produced by Smart Brothers of Brierley Hill. Single and multiple flower tubes imitating bamboo were also made by a number of firms. These 'rustic' style decorations remained popular well into the twentieth century. An eccentric series of 'rustic' decorations, incorporating the rose, thistle and shamrock, and the letters 'E.R' and 'A.R', were produced by John Walsh Walsh to commemorate the Coronation of King Edward and Queen Alexandra and are

106 Centrepiece in straw opaline glass, with furnace-wrought applied trails, barley sugar twists and handles in clear glass. Probably made in the Stourbridge area. *c.* 1895–1900. h. 22$^{1}/_{2}$ in. *Victoria & Albert Museum.*

illustrated in the *Pottery Gazette* (May 1902). Even as late as 1915, Mrs Beeton's *Book of Household Management* recommends the use of 'rustic' table decorations, remarking that they are 'extremely pretty although rather old-fashioned'.

In the late 1880s and 1890s many firms produced naturalistic flower stands imitating actual flowers and plants. As early as 1886 John Walsh Walsh produced fairy lights mounted on a naturalistic water-lily leaf which they registered as their 'Water-Lily Glass'. This registration was followed in 1888 with an even more realistic water-lily and bud mounted on a leaf, which in turn was imitated by other firms, including Thomas Webb & Sons, who in 1891 registered an elaborate series of table decorations incorporating water-lilies and swans with trumpet vases. In May 1888 John Walsh Walsh registered a series of palm trees of varying heights up to thirty inches which were made with ruby stems and crystal leaves, or, alternatively, entirely in crystal. The *Pottery Gazette* (September 1890), describes this firm's latest novelties, among them a moss rose in ruby and white glass mounted on an amber stem, the stems and leaves being made to stand flat upon the table. Similar tea roses were made with green leaves. These roses could be used singly, one at each place setting, or combined into larger composite flower stands by the use of metal supports. Other naturalistic flower stands by John Walsh Walsh included a 'Thistle' flower stand (1888), a 'Crocus' (1891), an 'Arum Lily' (1896) and 'Foxglove' (1898). The most attractive of their table decorations is perhaps the water-lily glass that they registered in 1903. The lilies are formed of opalescent glass, with opaque ribs, and natural green leaves, supported by brass stems. These are more graceful and elegant than the earlier flowers and are in keeping with the current art nouveau style. These decorations by John Walsh Walsh were on a fairly popular level but the high class Stourbridge firms of H. G. Richardson & Sons and Thomas Webb also catered for this taste. In 1898 Richardson's registered their miniature fir cones in opalescent glass with rustic branches in crystal. These were used singly or built up into multiple flower stands and a number of them are illustrated in the *Pottery Gazette* (June 1898). The fir cones were followed by the 'Campanula' series in December 1898, which had bell-shaped flowers similarly set on rustic work, either singly or in groups of up to a dozen flowers. The flowers were made in opalescent glass with a tinge of mauve, blue, or

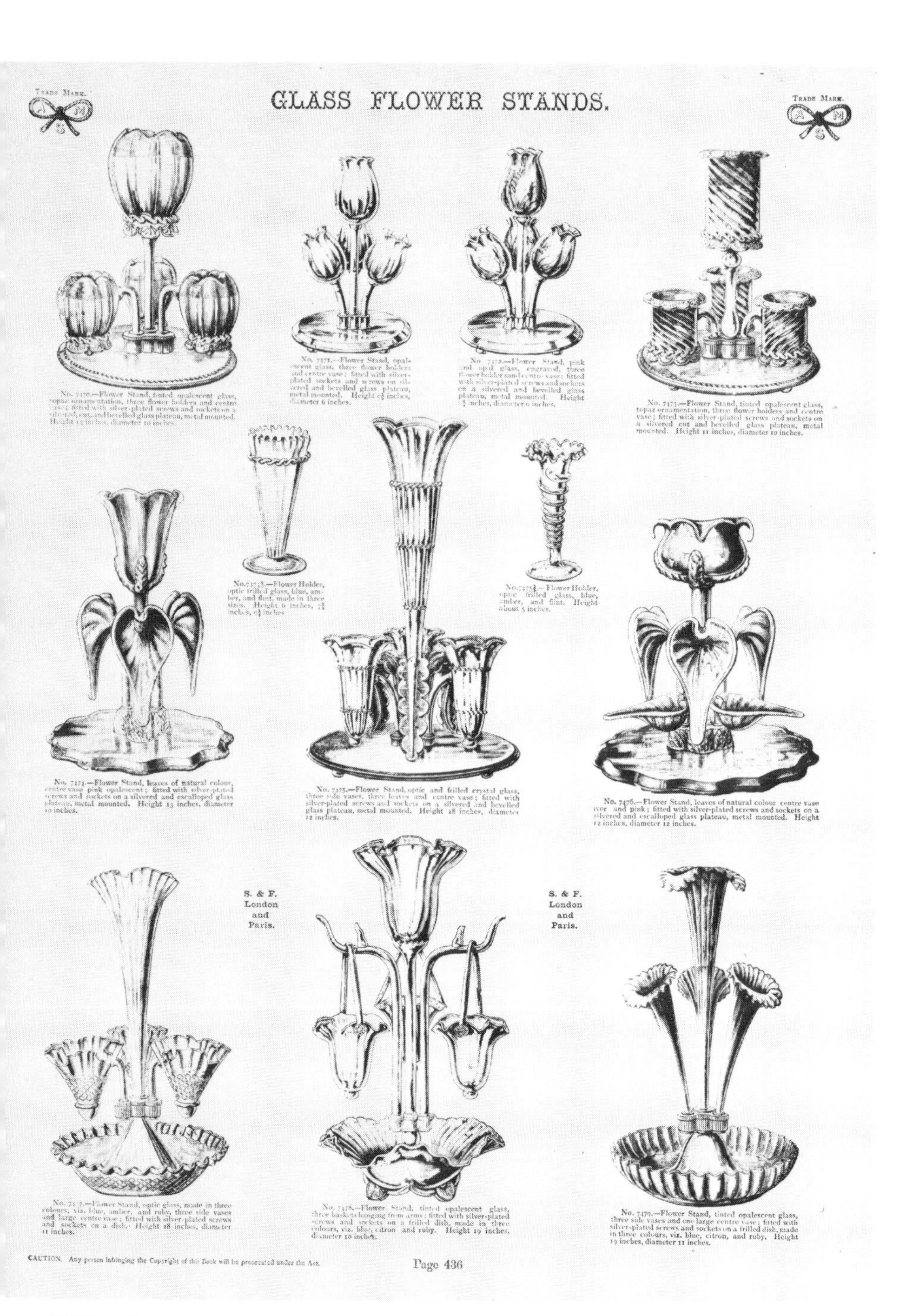

Trade Mark.

GLASS FLOWER STANDS.

Trade Mark.

No. 7170.—Flower Stand, tinted opalescent glass, topaz ornamentation, three flower holders and centre vase; fitted with silver-plated screws and sockets on a silvered, cut, and bevelled glass plateau, metal mounted. Height 14 inches, diameter 10 inches.

No. 7171.—Flower Stand, opalescent glass, three flower holders and centre vase; fitted with silver-plated sockets and screws on silvered and bevelled glass plateau, metal mounted. Height 9¾ inches, diameter 6 inches.

No. 7172.—Flower Stand, pink and opal glass, engraved, three flower holders and centre vase; fitted with silver-plated screws and sockets on a silvered and bevelled glass plateau, metal mounted. Height [illegible]¼ inches, diameter 6 inches.

No. 7173.—Flower Stand, tinted opalescent glass, topaz ornamentation, three flower holders and centre vase; fitted with silver-plated screws and sockets on a silvered cut and bevelled glass plateau, metal mounted. Height 11 inches, diameter 10 inches.

No. 7174.—Flower Stand, leaves of natural colour, centre vase pink opalescent; fitted with silver-plated screws and sockets on a silvered and escalloped glass plateau, metal mounted. Height 13 inches, diameter 10 inches.

No. 7175¼.—Flower Holder, optic frilled glass, blue, amber, and flint, made in three sizes. Height 6 inches, 7¼ inches, 9¼ inches.

No. 7175.—Flower Stand, optic and frilled crystal glass, three side vases, three leaves and centre vase; fitted with silver-plated screws and sockets on a silvered and bevelled glass plateau, metal mounted. Height 18 inches, diameter 12 inches.

No. 7175½.—Flower Holder, optic frilled glass, blue, amber, and flint. Height about 5 inches.

No. 7476.—Flower Stand, leaves of natural colour centre vase ivor and pink; fitted with silver-plated screws and sockets on a silvered and escalloped glass plateau, metal mounted. Height 12 inches, diameter 12 inches.

S. & F.
London
and
Paris.

S. & F.
London
and
Paris.

No. 71[illegible]7.—Flower Stand, optic glass, made in three colours, viz. blue, amber, and ruby, three side vases and large centre vase; fitted with silver-plated screws and sockets on a dish. Height 18 inches, diameter 11 inches.

No. 7178.—Flower Stand, tinted opalescent glass, three baskets hanging from arms; fitted with silver-plated screws and sockets on a frilled dish, made in three colours, viz. blue, citron and ruby. Height 19 inches, diameter 10 inches.

No. 7179.—Flower Stand, tinted opalescent glass, three side vases and one large centre vase; fitted with silver-plated screws and sockets on a frilled dish, made in three colours, viz. blue, citron, and ruby. Height 19 inches, diameter 11 inches.

Page 436

107 Page from a Silber & Fleming catalogue of 1889.

SILBER & FLEMING'S GLASS TABLE ORNAMENTS, WITH OR WITHOUT FLOWERS.

TRADE MARK

5029 Jardinière, formed of crystal glass bars, strongly bound together with silver-plated wire, supporting a boat-shaped glass receptacle for natural or artificial flowers. The plateau is of silvered glass with bevelled edge, mounted on a solid base, covered with maroon-coloured velvet. Dimensions of Jardinière—Height, 4 inches; length, 18¼ inches; width 4¾ inches. Dimensions of Plateau—Length, 17 inches; width 7¾ inches, thickness about 1 inch. Price complete, 16/6 each

5018 Jardinière, oblong shape with square ends, formed of crystal glass bars, strongly bound together with silver-plated wire. The Jardinière stands upon a silvered glass plateau with cut bevelled edge, mounted on a solid base, which is covered with maroon-coloured velvet. Dimensions of Jardinière, height, 3 ins.; length, 10 ins.; width, 3½ ins. Dimensions of Plateau, length, 13 ins.; width, 6 ins.; thickness about 1 in. Price complete, 13/6 each

5019 Jardinière, octagon shape, formed of crystal glass bars, strongly bound together with silver-plated wire. The Jardinière stands upon a round plateau of silvered glass, with cut bevelled edge, mounted on a solid base, which is covered with maroon-coloured velvet. Dimensions of Jardinière, height, 3½ ins.; diameter, 11 ins. Dimensions of Plateau, diameter 14½ ins.; thickness about 1 inch. Price complete, £1 5s. each

5009 Flower Holder, threaded glass shell, blue, opalescent, citron or rose colour, fixed on a silvered glass plateau with cut bevelled edge and metal mount. Height 2¾ ins., diameter 4 ins., 39/ per doz.

5011 Flower Holder, threaded glass shell, turquoise, opalescent, citron or rose colour, fixed on an oval silvered glass plateau with cut bevelled edge and metal mount. Height 3½ inches, length 4 inches, 30/ per doz.

No. 4922 Jardinière, oblong, formed of silvered and bevelled glass panels, supported by crystal glass bars, ornamented with glass chains and pendants. The Jardinière contains a movable metal box, for holding flowers or ferns, and stands upon a plateau of silvered glass, with cut bevelled edge, mounted on a solid base, which is covered with maroon-coloured velvet. Jardinière—height about 10½ inches; length about 9 inches; width about 4½ inches. Plateau—length about 14 inches, width about 10 inches, complete 30/ each

ALL PRICES ARE QUOTED WITHOUT FLOWERS.
WHEN ORDERING PLEASE STATE IF YOU WISH FLOWERS FOR EACH ORNAMENT.

IMITATION FLOWERS FROM 5/ TO 30/ EXTRA FOR EACH ORNAMENT, ACCORDING TO SIZE OF ORNAMENT AND QUALITY OF FLOWERS.

TRADE MARK

5033 Jardinière, sexagon shape, formed of six silvered, engraved, and bevelled glass panels, supported by six crystal glass bars with ball tops. The Jardinière contains a movable metal box for holding natural or artificial plants, ferns, or flowers, and stands upon a silvered glass plateau with bevelled edge, mounted on a solid base, which is covered with maroon-coloured velvet. Dimensions of Jardinière, height 7 inches, diameter 7¾ inches. Dimensions of Plateau, diameter 12 inches, thickness about 1 inch. Price complete, £1 10s. each

5034 Jardinière, diamond shaped, formed of four silvered, engraved, and bevelled glass panels, supported by four crystal glass bars. The Jardinière contains a movable metal box for holding natural or artificial plants, ferns, or flowers, and stands upon a plateau of silvered glass with cut bevelled edge, mounted on a solid base, which is covered with maroon-coloured velvet. Dimensions of Jardinière, height 7 inches; length, 14 inches; width, 9 inches. Dimensions of Plateau, length 19 inches; width 14 inches; thickness about 1 inch. Price complete £2 5s. each

108 Page from a Silber & Fleming catalogue of 1889.

flint and yellow. The productions of Thomas Webb were perhaps more sophisticated and conventional. For example, a multiple flower stand registered by Thomas Webb in February 1891, has six tall trumpet-shaped vases with flower-like tops and a calyx at the base, set asymetrically on slender stems about the central support which has a spreading foot. From 1886 onwards, Thomas Webb were also very active in the production of table decorations that incorporated Samuel Clarke's Patent 'Fairy Lights' in their Queen's Burmese Ware. These included single pyramid lamps of the familiar acorn shape, set in a small bowl with a crimped edge, which could hold cut flowers. Others were adapted to hold menu cards. Elaborate centrepieces, with bowls for fruit and flowers, and flower vases, with a group of fairy lights, were also made in Burmese glass, the designs being registered by Clarke's rather than Webb's. Clarke's also used Webb's Burmese lamps with bowls of Doulton's 'Tapestry' ware. Flower bowls containing a single fairy lamp were made by other Stourbridge firms in every conceivable type of fancy glass – satin, *nacre de perle* threaded opaline, various types of 'pull-up' decoration – as well as in cut flint glass. The *Pottery Gazette* (July 1886), illustrates a particularly elaborate combined centrepiece and candelabra in satin and crystal glass. A five 'Fairy' light candelabra is set on an elaborate rustic crystal stem and base decorated with applied leaves and flowers. This rests on a mirror plateau on a velvet-covered base which has three flower bowls in satin glass similarly decorated with applied leaves and flowers. Similar table decorations to the 'Fairy' light, made exclusively by Edward Webb, White House Glass Works, Wordsley, were called the 'Will-o-the-Wisp' illuminated flower bowls. The shades were larger than those of the 'Fairy' lights and were in the shape of a vase, narrowing towards the neck, with a flaring crimped top, and were made in a wide variety of fancy glass.

Another form of table decoration introduced about 1870 and popular throughout the 1880s and 1890s consisted of narrow flower troughs of pressed glass with straight, vertically ribbed sides. They were made in a wide variety of shapes and sizes – oblong, cruciform, circular, semi-circular, etc. – and could be combined in different ways on a mirror plateau. Miniature glass lifeboats, in varying sizes, the sides patterned to imitate the 'brilliant' style of cutting, first registered by Henry Greener, Sunderland, in 1887, were produced by a number of firms for use as flower holders. They were supported either by a block of crystal glass cut with slots in which the boat rested, or by a framework of glass tubes, held together by silver wire, the whole standing on a mirror plateau. Glass swans, first registered by Hodgetts & Richardson in 1872, were similarly employed, together with wheelbarrows, glass shoes, Venetian gondolas, and other novelties. It seems there was no limit to the ingenuity of the glass manufacturers in producing an endless stream of novelties for table decoration. There is little doubt, however, that the symmetrical flower stand with a central trumpet-shaped vase and subsidiary vases or hanging baskets, developed in the late 1860s and 1870s, remained the most popular, continuing in fashion until about 1924. Unfortunately, owing to their extreme fragility, relatively few in relation to the enormous quantity produced have survived intact, and many extant examples have been 'cannibalised' and altered.

CHAPTER 10

AESTHETIC AND ARTS AND CRAFTS GLASS

THE intellectual approach of the Arts and Crafts movement to the design of glass had its theoretical basis in the works of John Ruskin (1814–1900) and the lectures of William Morris (1834–1896). Ruskin and Morris were united in their condemnation of most of the current fashionable styles in table glass and recommended a return to the methods of the sixteenth- and seventeenth-century Venetian glassworkers. In *The Stones of Venice* (vol. II, 1853, Chapter VI, p. 168) Ruskin writes:

> Our modern glass is exquisitely clear in its substance, true in its form, accurate in its cutting. We are proud of this. We ought to be ashamed of it. The old Venice glass was muddy, inaccurate in all its forms, and clumsily cut if at all. And the old Venetian was justly proud of it. For there is this difference between the English and Venetian workman, that the former thinks only of accurately matching his patterns, getting his curves perfectly true and his edges perfectly sharp and becomes a mere machine for rounding curves and shaping edges, while the old Venetian cared not a whit whether his edges were sharp or not, but he invented a new design for every glass he made, and never moulded a handle or a lip without a new fancy in it.

Later on in the same volume (Appendix 12, pp. 391–2) Ruskin stresses the importance of respecting the qualities of glass as a material: 'The workman has not done his duty and is not working on safe principles, unless he even so far *honours* the materials with which he is working as to set himself to bring out their beauty, and to

109 Claret jug of engraved glass mounted in silver plate with an ivory handle. The mount bears a diamond registry mark and the letters 'H & H' indicating that it was registered by Hukin & Heath, Birmingham, 9 May 1881. Designed by (or under the supervision of) Dr Christopher Dresser. h. $8^1/_4$ in. *Private collection.*

recommend and exalt, as far as he can, their peculiar qualities . . . he will invariably find the material grateful, and that his work is all the nobler for being eulogistic of the substance of which it is made. But of all the arts, the working of glass is that in which we ought to keep these principles most vigorously in mind'.

According to Ruskin the two chief characteristics of glass are:

> its DUCTILITY when heated and its TRANSPARENCY when cold, both nearly perfect. In its employment for vessels, we ought always to exhibit its ductility, and in its employment for windows its transparency. All work in glass is bad which does not, with loud voice, proclaim one or other of these great qualities. Consequently, *all cut glass* is barbarous: for the cutting conceals its ductility, and confuses it with crystal. Also all very neat, finished and perfect form in glass is barbarous: for this fails in proclaiming another of its great virtues; namely the ease with which its light substance can be moulded or blown into any form so long as perfect accuracy be not required . . . no delicate outlines are to be attempted, but only such fantastic fickle grace as the mind of the workman can conceive and execute on the instant. The more wild, extravagant and grotesque in their gracefulness the forms are, the better. No material is so adapted for giving full play to the imagination but it must not be wrought with refinement or painfulness, still less with costliness. For as in gratitude we proclaim its virtues, so in all honesty are we to confess its imperfections; and while we triumphantly set forth its transparency, we are frankly to admit its fragility, and therefore not waste too much time upon it, nor put any real art into it when intended for daily use. No workman ought ever to spend more than an hour in the making of any glass vessel.

For Ruskin, it was as much a moral question as an aesthetic one. He believed that beautiful things could be made only by those who had joy in their work . . . 'Beautiful art can only be produced by people who have beautiful things about them, and leisure to look at them, and unless you provide some elements of beauty for your workman to be surrounded by, you will find that no elements of beauty can be invented by them' (Lecture on 'Modern Manufacture and Design' delivered at Bradford, March 1859 and printed in *The Two Paths*, London, 1859, p. 90).

Ruskin was disturbed at the divorce of the designer from the actual production and, although he recognised – particularly in large-scale production – the necessity for one man's thought being carried out by the labours of others, his ideal was where the designer and executant were one and the same. Above all he respected the dignity of labour and insisted that work must be a pleasure if any good was to come out of it.

William Morris followed closely on Ruskin in his ideas on art and design but he was to go further than Ruskin, believing that only a fundamental change to a truly socialist society could bring about a true revival of art. He had the same moral attitude as Ruskin, believing that beauty was unobtainable except as the expression of man's joy in his everyday labour, work that would produce articles that were 'a joy to the maker and to the user'.

William Morris's views on the design of glass echo Ruskin's in every detail and are most clearly set out in his lecture on 'The Lesser Arts of Life' delivered in support of the Society for the Protection of Ancient Buildings in 1882 (*Collected Works*, vol. XXII, 1914). His condemnation of current production is perhaps even more vehement than Ruskin's:

110 Carafe with engraved decoration from the 'Prince of Wales Service' made by Apsley Pellatt. 1862. h. $6^7/_8$ in. *Royal Scottish Museum, Edinburgh.*

111 A group of table glass designed by Philip Webb for Morris, Marshall, Faulkner & Company and made by James Powell & Sons, Whitefriars, from 1861. *Victoria & Albert Museum.*

Never till our own day has an ugly or stupid glass vessel been made; and no wonder, considering the capabilities of the art. In the hands of a good workman the metal is positively alive, and is, you may say, coaxing him to make something pretty. Nothing but commercial enterprise capturing the unlucky man and setting him down in the glass-maker's chair with his pattern book beside him (which I should think must generally have been originally designed by a landscape gardener); nothing but this kind of thing could turn out ugly glasses. This stupidity will never be set right till we give up demanding accurately-gauged classes by the gross. I am fully in earnest when I say that if I were setting about getting good glasses made I would get some good workmen together, tell them the height and capacity of the vessels I wanted, and perhaps some general idea as to shape, and then let them do their best. . .

112 Jug and tumbler in clear glass designed by Philip Webb for Morris, Marshall, Faulkner & Company and made by James Powell & Sons, Whitefriars, from 1861. h. $4^3/_4$ in. and $3^3/_4$ in. *Museum Bellerive, Zürich.*

113 Three drinking glasses with twisted stems and applied green prunts. Made by James Powell & Sons, Whitefriars. Based on designs by Philip Webb of about 1860. *c.* 1900. h. $6^1/_4$ in., 7 in. and $6^3/_4$ in. *Museum Bellerive, Zürich.*

> In speaking of glass-work, it is a matter of course that I am only thinking of that which is blown and worked by hand; moulded and cut glass may have commercial but cannot have artistic value. . . Modern managers have worked very hard to get their glass colourless; it does not seem to me that they have quite succeeded. I should say that their glass was cold and bluish in colour; but whether or not, their aim was wrong. A slight tint is an advantage in the metal; so are slight specks and streaks, for these things make the form visible.

Morris goes on to praise Venetian glass of the seventeenth century:

> This glass of Venice and Murano is most delicate in its form, and was certainly meant quite as much for ornament as use; so you may be sure that if the makers of it had seen any necessity for getting more mechanical perfection in their metal they would have tried for it and got it; but like all true artists they were contented when they had a material that suited the purpose of their special craft, and would not weary themselves in seeking after what they did not want. And I feel sure if they had been making glass for ordinary table use at a low price, and which ran more risks of breakage, as they would have had to fashion their vessels thicker and less daintily they would have been contented with a rougher metal than that which they used. Such a manufacture yet remains to be set on foot, and I very much wish it could be done; only it must be done by hand, and not by machine, human or otherwise.

Although he was an exact contemporary of William Morris, being born in the same year, Dr Christopher Dresser (1834–1904) was, in contrast to Morris, primarily an industrial designer, designing for mass production by machine. His views on table glass nevertheless coincided very much with those of Ruskin and Morris, though his approach was from a functional rather than an aesthetic or moral point of view. He was one of the first freelance professional designers to succeed in breaking through the traditional anonymity of the decorative artist. The glass that he designed in the late 1870s and early 1880s was functional rather than aesthetic – simple claret jugs, decanters and tumblers, of which the silver-mounts, executed by Birmingham silversmiths such as Hukin & Heath, were even more avant-garde and twentieth century in appearance than the simple shapes they supported (Plate 109). He was, however, an extremely influential writer on design and his views no doubt contributed to the fashion for simple, plain glass advocated by aesthetic devotees. His views are set out most clearly in the chapter devoted to hollow vessels in his *Principles of Decorative Design*, first published in 1873. Like Ruskin and Morris he stressed the importance of respecting the fluidity of glass in its molten state and exploiting its natural properties:

> Let a portion of molten glass be gathered upon the end of a metal pipe, and blown into a bubble while the pipe drops vertically from the mouth of the operator, and a flask is formed such as is used for the conveyance of olive oil; and what vessel could be more beautiful than such a flask? Its grace of form is obvious, the delicate curvature of its sides, the gentle swelling of the bulb, and the exquisitely rounded base, all manifest beauty. . . . Here we get a vessel formed for us almost wholly by Nature.

But when he came to conscious design, two basic principles stood out to Dresser as all-important: firstly, that the material should be worked in the manner most befitting to its nature; and secondly, the

114 Decanter and stopper of clear green glass designed by Sir T. G. Jackson (1835–1924) in 1874 and made for James Powell & Sons, Whitefriars. h. 9 in. *Victoria & Albert Museum.*

115 Ribbed liqueur decanter and stopper with blue glass trailing made by James Powell & Sons, Whitefriars. *c.* 1890. In the possession of the makers. h. 10⁷/₈ in. *Photograph Victoria & Albert Museum.*

116 'Leather Bottle' decanter of clear glass with trailed and pincered decoration. Made by many firms in the late 19th century. h. 8 in. *Victoria & Albert Museum.*

consideration of the purpose the object to be formed is intended to serve. There follows a detailed examination of what a decanter should be with the conclusion that 'if we take a flask and flatten its base, and extend the upper part of the neck slightly into the form of a funnel, we have all that is required of a decanter, with the exception of a permanent cork, which is a stopper . . . But as most decanters are intended to hold wine, it is desirable to give the vessel a foot, or, in other words, raise the body of the decanter so that light may surround it as fully as possible'. He points out that many other things are formed of glass – tumblers, wine glasses, flower holders, etc. – but that the same basic principles apply to all – 'if the objects formed result from the easiest method of working the material, and are such as perfectly answer the end proposed by their formation, and are beautiful, nothing more can be expected of them'.

On the subject of cut glass he states that 'cutting may be employed in bringing about ornamental effects on glass, but it is rarely to be commended when so lavishly used as to be the chief means of giving form to the vessel; indeed, cutting should be sparingly and judici-

117 'Clutha' vase of green glass, bubbled and streaked, designed by Christopher Dresser and made by James Couper & Sons, Glasgow. Marked 'CLUTHA – DESIGNED BY C.D. REGISTERED' and with a flower device. Late 1880s. h. 5 in. *Victoria & Albert Museum.*

ously used. A vessel formed of glass should never be wholly shaped by cutting as though it were a work of stone. If the neck of a decanter can be made more convenient by being slightly cut – if it can be so treated that it can be held more securely – then let it be cut'. Similarly, he held that engraving should also be somewhat sparingly used, and, as an example in good taste, illustrated a decanter from the Prince of Wales service made by Apsley Pellatt (Plate 110).

Yet another influential writer whose views on table glass coincided with those of Ruskin and Morris was Charles Lock Eastlake (1836–1906). His *Hints on Household Taste*, first published in book form in 1868, contains a chapter on 'Table Glass'. Like Ruskin and Morris, Eastlake stressed the necessity for respecting the natural properties of glass, recognising its ductability and fluidity. He regarded the glass produced in Venice in the fifteenth, sixteenth and seventeenth centuries as the ideal and attacked the English lead crystal for its very perfection: 'If it is to be perfectly colourless and clear as water, but heavy withal, then Modern English glass is the best that has been produced. But to the eye of an artist the delicate graduations of natural colour, the slight imperfections and streakiness of old glass, render it infinitely more attractive than a purity of texture which has nothing but its clearness to recommend it.' Eastlake, however, considered that an improvement had already taken place since the 1851 Exhibition:

> People began to discover that the round bulbous form of decanter was a more pleasant object to look at than the rigid outline of a pseudo-crystal pint pot carved and chopped about into unnecessary grooves and planes. The reversed and truncated cone, which served our grandfathers for wine glasses, gradually disappeared before the lily and crocus shaped bowls from which we now sip our sherry and Bordeaux. Champagne had formerly been drunk from tall and narrow glasses . . . it is now a broad and shallow *tazza* which sparkles with the vintage of Epernay. For some years past the forms of our goblets and water-bottles have been gradually improving; many artistic varieties of the material have appeared, and the style of decoration employed, especially with engraved glass, is very superior to what it used to be.

Eastlake mentions the fact that some English glass manufacturers have endeavoured to reproduce old Venetian glass, but he regards

118 Two 'Clutha' vases of green glass streaked in colours and aventurine designed by George Walton for James Couper & Sons, Glasgow. *c.* 1896. h. 3 in. and 3½ in. *Victoria & Albert Museum.*

their productions as inferior to those of Dr Salviati in Venice.

Although Eastlake designed furniture, and a few textiles and wallpapers, he did not design any glass, nor did Morris. The first glassware that corresponded to these theories was that designed by Philip Webb (1831–1915), the architect friend and associate of William Morris.

Of the table glass designed by Philip Webb, the most elaborate was that designed for William Morris's personal use at Red House, the house Webb built for him at Bexley Heath. A sheet of original designs for this glass is in the Victoria & Albert Museum and is inscribed 'Designs for Glass Vessels for W. Morris Esq.' and signed 'P. Webb, archt. 7 Gt Ormond St Jan 7 1860'. The service consisted of four water jugs, six large drinking glasses, thirty goblets, thirty large wine glasses and thirty small, two grace cups, four decanters and four flower vases. The designs, which are executed in pencil, ink and watercolour, are very 'medieval' in spirit and are somewhat reminiscent of German drinking glasses of the sixteenth century.

The water jug is very medieval in shape, with a robust handle and a high flaring lip, richly enamelled in white, brown and gold in horizontal bands with blue spots. The tall large drinking glass is similarly enamelled and is very Germanic in shape, with a domed foot. The water glass is a simple tumbler with threaded decoration described as 'a small spiral worm'. The goblet also has bands of threaded decoration and the stem, which is sexfoil in section, is twisted about a quarter round. The large wine glass is in the form of a simple rummer and the smaller wine glass, which has a waved outline at the base of the bowl, has a twisted quatrefoil stem. The designs for the grace cup, decanter and flower vase are not included on the sheet and do not appear to have survived. Nor, indeed, does the actual glass.

Webb also designed a considerable range of much simpler table glass that was made by Powell's of Whitefrairs and sold by Morris, Marshall, Faulkner & Company in the early days of the firm, which was founded in April 1861. Philip Webb's passbook for 1862–78 (in the possession of John Brandon-Jones, Esq.) includes thumbnail sketches of a number of the items. Some of the entries concern the price paid to Webb for his original designs: '20 designs for wine glasses at 5/– and ditto for tumblers': 'design for water cruet & tumbler, finger glass, liqueur glass, sugar basin £2', and 'jam dish & cover 10/–'; other entries show glasses taken by Webb from the firm's stock in part payment for his services.

From the thumbnail sketches, further original designs in the Victoria & Albert Museum, and from the records at Powell's, there seem to have been several distinct ranges. The most interesting and original is perhaps that characterised by a convex bulge, or waved outline, as the only decoration to an otherwise simple basic shape. This occurs in a tumbler, a tall stemmed glass, a kind of rummer, a finger bowl, sugar basin and a water jug (Plates 111, 112). The latter is of particular interest in that the handle, instead of being in line with the lip, is placed at a right angle to it. It is also worth noting that the water tumbler, with minor modifications, has survived to this day as a common type of public house beer glass.

Another range of two goblets and a rummer (for which the designs are in the Victoria & Albert Museum) have the quatrefoil section, quarter-twisted stem found in the designs for William Morris. The Powell records also show a water jug, rummer and two tumblers with spiral threaded decoration. The Victoria & Albert Museum designs also include five tall champagne glasses with trumpet and tulip shaped bowls on tall stems ornamented with a merese, or angular bladed knop between the bowl and the stem (Plate 111).

A particularly original shape, described in the passbook as 'a church glass' has a simple cylindrical bucket-shaped bowl, ornamental with green glass beads at the base, on a tall slender stem with a plain conical foot. Many slight modifications of this design were produced by Powell's later in the century, a particularly pleasing variant having a lilac stem and lilac beads (Plate 113). A number of the other Webb designs were also revived by Powell's in the early twentieth century.

In the 1860s, however, the glass made by Powell's to Webb's designs seems to have been sold exclusively by Morris & Company, and Powell's normal range was similar to that of other high-class glass-houses such as Apsley Pellatt and some of the Stourbridge firms. In the 1870s, however, Powell's embarked on what may be

119 Two goblets and a tumbler in streaky green glass, lamp-blown, made by James Ranken Garrow, Glasgow. *c.* 1900. *Victoria & Albert Museum.*

termed 'aesthetic glass' on their own account. In 1874 they commissioned designs from another architect T. G. Jackson (later Sir Thomas Graham Jackson, Bart.) which had a comparable simplicity to that designed by Webb, but which was mostly made in a pale green glass. The decanter shown in Plate 114 with its band of furnace wrought decoration and disc stopper, recalls the shaft and globe decanters of the early eighteenth century. A wine glass and a tall wide-bowled champagne glass were designed to match. An oval claret decanter, with trailed and pincered decoration, had been introduced some years earlier, probably, about 1865; the shape was copied from an ancient leather bottle. These shapes remained in production for many years, and were copied by a number of other firms (Plate 116).

Other designs by James Powell and Sons in pale green glass were mentioned by the *Pottery Gazette* (October 1877, p. 53): 'In water jugs we noted one in shape resembling the ewers found by Dr Schliemann at Mycenae'. They also produced a range decorated with pale blue threading, including wine glasses with blue threading round the lower half of the bowl which were described by the *Pottery Gazette* in the same article as 'among the handsomest we have seen'. The liqueur decanter shown in Plate 115 is a good example of this style.

Comparable to the simple shapes in table glass designed by Philip Webb and T. G. Jackson, was the 'Munstead' range of flower glasses designed by the gardening expert Gertrude Jekyll (1843–1932) in 1884 and named after her Surrey home. Gertrude Jekyll was a friend and admirer of Ruskin and it was not surprising that she strongly disapproved of the elaborate, often brightly coloured, flower vases and centrepieces that were currently in fashion. Her solution was to design a range of flower holders which she considered would set off the flowers she so dearly loved in all their natural beauty. The range consisted of about a dozen shapes of bowls and vases made in varying sizes, some designed to be set in groups down the centre of a long dinner table, others to be used at each place setting. These 'Munstead Glasses', as they were called, are fully described in an article in *The Garden* (29 March 1884, p. 248) and a photograph of some of them appears in her book, *Home and Garden*, first published in 1900. They were sold exclusively by James Green & Nephew of Queen Victoria Street and were probably made by Powell's of Whitefriars. The range was intended to hold every variety of flowers and foliage 'from a bunch of Violets to the largest decoration that can be put on a table'. They were made in clear, untinted glass and were 'strong, low in price and capable of holding a large quantity of water'.

The simple shapes designed by T. G. Jackson, some of the Venetian imitations, and other glass by Powell's, were strongly recommended by Mrs Loftie in *The Dining Room*, one of the volumes in the Macmillan 'Art at Home' series, published in 1878. All these volumes propagated the artistic home with Morris wallpapers and the 'Queen Anne Style' decoration and furniture favoured by the architect Richard Norman Shaw. The volumes were aimed at the middle classes rather than the wealthy. Venetian glass was approved of but considered too expensive and fragile for the average home. The book illustrates in outline some of the table glass in the Powell range, which was praised for good form and was considered to be in much better taste than the 'cast and moulded atrocities which have hitherto monopolised the cheap market'. The prevalent habit of having everything in matching sets was considered unnecessary; indeed, the writer considered different shapes for the various glasses, decanters and carafes even desirable for the sake of variety – 'refreshing where it does not banish harmony'.

This 'aesthetic' type of glass was in considerable demand in the late 1870s. A correspondent to the *Pottery Gazette* (October 1879), signing himself 'An Old Fogy', grumbles at 'the present flimsy glass that decorates our tables, such as etched, spun, twisted, Venetian and other abortions that meet us at nearly every dinner table. Where is the elegant, brilliant cut glass that used to set off our silver and our damask cloth? Gone. I fear it has given way to the fashion of the age – the flimsy fashion of 1879'.

The *Pottery Gazette* itself, which had highly praised the artistic glass in Powell's exhibit at Paris in 1878 had by 1882 turned against it: 'It is evident that the *plain era* in glass is dying out; plain wines and clarets as well as plain decanters are doomed, and the brilliant period is coming in again. At least let us hope that aestheticism is on the wane as far as glass is concerned for it means no labour, and as little trade, and certainly very little taste'. (1 February 1882, p. 145) Again, on 1 December 1882, the *Pottery Gazette* returns to the attack: 'The age of plain glass is gone or going, and good cut and engraved glass is fast coming in again, in spite of Dr Dresser & Oscar Wilde.'

Although the aesthetic movement as such had by this time passed its peak, the type of glass introduced by Powell's continued to attract a discerning public. Harry J. Powell (1853–1922) joined the firm in August 1875 and from 1880 the firm's production came under his direct control. Throughout his long working life H. J. Powell remained faithful to the ideals of Morris and the Arts and Crafts movement. He remained active in the firm until about 1920 and his book *History of Glass Making in England* was published in Cambridge 1923, shortly after his death.

An interesting scrap book, containing some of his original sketches, and design reference material in the form of photographs of nature illustrations from periodicals and various odd jottings, is preserved in the firm's archives. It includes a series of simple plant drawings, dated 1893 and 1898, rather after the manner of the woodcut illustrations in old herbals. These were used for the decoration of some tall engraved vases (similar to those in the 'Munstead' range) and decanters, each flower being used with an appropriate motto in English or French, or even Latin and Greek. Among them were five vases engraved as follows: 'Honeysuckle – *Tibi Dulcia*

120 Group of glass designed by George Walton and made by Venetian glassworkers at Earl's Court. 1904. h. 11½ in., 13 in. and 11 in. *Victoria & Albert Museum.*

Affero'; 'Speed-well!'; 'There is Pansies – That's for Thoughts'. 'Columbine – *L'Avant Courrière du Bon Temps*'; 'A Sweet Pea Blossom for Old Sake's Sake' and 'Shepherd's Purse – A Light Heart & a Full Purse'. A group of these vases was shown at the Manchester Arts and Crafts Exhibition of 1895. In the 1890s this use of mottoes was prevalent in the Arts and Crafts movement; we find them used appropriately in embroidery, on beaten copper and pewter, to decorate pottery and porcelain, even on furniture and as a wall frieze decoration.

This scrap book also includes some designs by Heywood Sumner (1853–1940), a prominent member of the Arts and Crafts Exhibition Society and the Art Workers' Guild. Three designs of a rose tree, tulip and poppy, dated 1898 and treated in a rather formal art nouveau style, were used by Powell's to decorate a series of tall goblets of flint glass, cut and polished, with an engraved and gilt bowl of an hexagonal conical form. At this period the chief engraver at Powell's was a Mr Hillebauer.

Harry Powell himself designed a number of highly original glass services which made an important contribution to the art nouveau style (Plate 121). Glasses with long slender stems and delicate bowls decorated with trailed decoration formed by melted-in threads, are typical of his work about the turn of the century. Others had three-strand twisted stems; some were decorated with sea-green prunts; others were given a curious misty texture by being rolled in platinum. The goblets he designed to commemorate the 1897 Diamond Jubilee were a far cry from the popular souvenirs produced by the firms specialising in pressed glass (see Chapter 11). The form is derived from Rhenish goblets of the sixteenth century. Indeed, a great deal of Harry Powell's energies (and those of James C. Powell) were devoted to the copying of glass of earlier periods, drawing inspiration from extant Museum specimens and the glasses depicted in Old Master paintings, such as the flower glass in the foreground of Hugo van der Goes's Portinari Altarpiece. For this purpose, Powell used soda lime glass as well as lead crystal. Not all these 'Old Master' glasses were direct copies; many of them combined features from a number of different historic prototypes, producing glass of a diverse and original character.

A detailed account of Powell's soda lime glass is given in an article by A. H. Church in *The Portfolio* for 1890 (p. 42). Soda lime glass had

121 Decanter and stopper with wheel-engraved decoration from the 'Lotus' service designed for the King of Siam in 1899 and made by James Powell & Sons, Whitefriars. *Private collection.*

been little used in this country but by diminishing the proportion of lime used and increasing that of the soda, Powell's produced a very satisfactory material. The exact formula was as follows: silica, 67·5 per cent; lime, 6·7 per cent; soda, 20·8 per cent; magnesia, 1·9 per cent; alumina, 2·5 per cent; with a trace of oxides of lead and iron and sulphuric acid. A group of soda lime glass – beakers, flasks, bowls and wine glasses – in honey-yellow, pale olive green, and aquamarine blue, was shown by Powell's at the Arts and Crafts Exhibition of 1889. The vessels felt light in the hand – indeed, a given bulk weighed little more than two-thirds of the same bulk of ordinary flint glass – but the glass was tough and hard. The shapes were simple and well-fitted for everyday use, and the inspiration was that of the seventeenth-century glass of the Low Countries. James C. Powell, brother of Harry Powell, visited museums in Holland and Belgium, making on the spot sketches, and also copies of glasses shown in Dutch and Flemish paintings. The glass blowers at Whitefriars worked direct from these sketches, producing not slavish copies, but glasses that very successfully captured the spirit of the originals.

About the turn of the century, Powell's produced a considerable number of claret jugs and decanters with silver mounts, mostly in the art nouveau style, which were similar to the silverwork of C. R. Ashbee and the Tudric pewter and Cymric silver of Liberty & Co. Indeed, Powell's supplied glass to Liberty's for their metalwork. The mounts were sometimes set with blister pearls or enriched with enamelling. The mounting was carried out by various silversmiths, including Hutton & Company of Birmingham and Ramsden & Carr.

Powell's glass featured regularly at the Arts and Crafts Exhibitions and was regarded as the result of individual craftsmanship rather than mere commercial production. Most of Powell's production was of the type that found favour with the Arts and Crafts movement, and it was sold regularly by Morris & Company. Somers Clarke in his essay on table glass (*Arts and Crafts Essays*, London, 1893) was as strong in his condemnation of heavy cut glass as Ruskin or Morris, describing the typical early Victorian cut-glass as 'a massive lump of mis-shapen material better suited to the purpose of braining a burglar than decorating a table'. He welcomed the trend for light and gracefully formed vessels. The 'Old Master' glasses of

Harry Powell were also approved – 'the works produced have been not merely copies, but they have their own character'.

A number of pieces of lamp-blown glass, designed and made by James Ranken Garrow (1870–1937) of Glasgow about 1900 may be compared to the art nouveau glasses of Harry Powell, but the glass is more eccentric in character and must be considered as experimental studio glass (Plate 119).

A rather different type of glass than can be grouped with 'aesthetic' and 'arts and crafts' glass, is the 'Clutha' glass of James Couper & Sons of Glasgow from the 1880s onwards. The first range was designed by Christopher Dresser, and each piece had this fact etched on the base (Plate 117). Some of the shapes were inspired by ancient Roman glass, others were more Persian in form and some were in a frankly eccentric, almost art nouveau style. The glass itself was deliberately bubbled and streaked, usually of a pale green colour, but sometimes bright pink or with slightly opaque or even red and bluish streaks. This type of glass was closely paralleled by Thomas Webb's 'Old Roman' which had a similar streaked and bubbled texture. Indeed, in 1888, Couper's complained that this glass by Webb's was a deliberate imitation of their 'Clutha' glass and a flagrant infringement of what they considered their copyright. In 1896 James Couper & Sons commissioned a new range of Clutha glass from the Glasgow architect George Walton (1867–1933). Some of these glasses were varied with patches of aventurine (Plate 118). George Walton later designed a set of clear green table glass, probably made by Powell's, which he exhibited at the Arts and Crafts Exhibition in 1903. The following year, at the Italian Exhibition at Earls Court, Venetian glass-blowers produced some fanciful covered vases to his design. Most of them were in clear glass, with furnace decoration and elaborately looped handles. Some of them had a bird on the cover or had decoration in deep blue glass and gilding (Plate 120).

CHAPTER 11

PRESSED GLASS

ONE of the great technical achievements of the Victorian glass manufacturers was the perfection of press-moulding to produce relief patterns by mechanical means. The use of moulds to determine shape and pattern goes back to Roman times, but it was not until the nineteenth century that the technique was commercially exploited to produce table and ornamental glass in huge quantities at a price which brought it within the means of every household.

In Great Britain, a primitive type of press-moulding had been used at the end of the eighteenth century for the solid bases of cut-glass bowls, goblets and salt cellars, and in the early nineteenth century glass was often blown into a one-piece mould to impart flutes to the lower part of a decanter or jug, which was otherwise to be decorated by cutting. Full-size two- or three-part moulds, which both shaped and patterned the vessel when the glass was blown into the mould, appear to have been widely in use, particularly for bottles, by the 1820s. This method was used extensively in the United States.

In glass-blowing by mouth the glass is gathered by dipping a hollow blowing iron into a pot of molten glass. This 'gather' cools to about 1,000 degrees Centigrade and then is 'marvered', that is rolled on an iron slab, to form a chilled layer on the outer surface which sustains the internal pressure of the glass-blower's breath as he blows down the tube, which in turn forms a cooled layer on the inner surface. When glass is blown into a mould, the mould works on the same principle of giving a cooled outer layer. When a relief pattern is obtained by the simple process of blowing a vessel into a mould, the

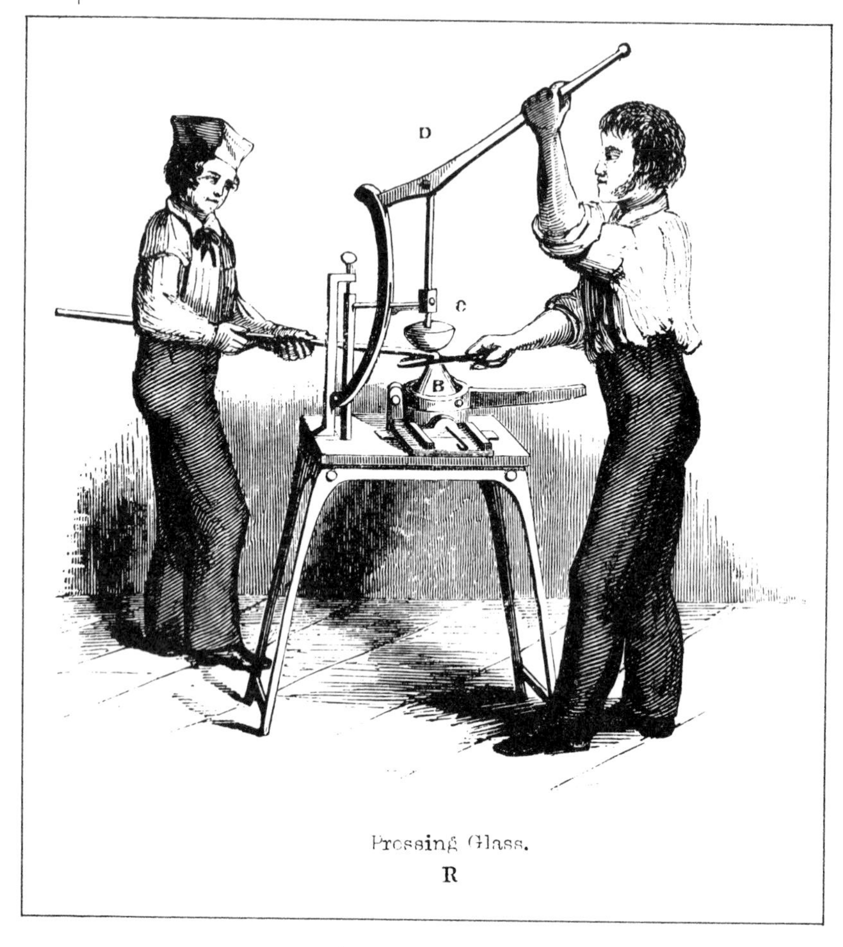

Pressing Glass.

R

pattern appears, as it were in reverse or negative, on the inside of the vessel, that is concave where it is convex on the outside, and vice-versa. An adaptation of mould-blowing, known as 'Pillar moulding' was used in the 1840s and is described by Apsley Pellatt in his *Curiosities of Glass Making*. It consisted of blowing into a part-sized mould a somewhat cooled gather of molten glass which had been given an outer coating of fully molten glass. Heavily protruding pillars of glass could thus be produced on the outside of the vessel with only slight irregularities on the inside. A catalogue of Apsley Pellatt and Company, dating from 1842, includes a large number of pillar-moulded dishes, finger cups, pickles, water carafes and tumblers.

Apart from its use for commercial bottle-making, mould-blowing continued to be used throughout the period (Plate 145), but with the development of press-moulding it was largely superseded as a method of producing cheap decorated table glass.

The process of forming articles in glass by pressing in a mould, a process which has remained virtually unchanged unto the present day, was commercially developed in the United States in the 1820s and introduced into Britain in the following decade. Briefly, the method was to press the required amount of molten glass for the article being made between a metal mould and a plunger, the inside of the mould being a negative of the outer surface of the article, and the outside of the plunger being the negative of the inside of the article. The process was suitable only for forming open-shaped objects – such as plates, dishes, bowls, tumblers and wide-necked jugs – from which the plunger could be withdrawn, although certain modifications in the shape of the pressed article could subsequently be made by manipulation. The surface of the glass in contact with the metal mould was slightly rough but a process of heat treatment known as 'fire-polishing' was used to obviate this defect. A good contemporary account of the exact methods of press-moulding is given in the *Newcastle Chronicle* (21 October 1882). It gives an account of operations at Sowerby & Company's Ellison Glass Works, in Gateshead, at that time the largest pressed-glass manufactory in the world, covering five acres and employing about a thousand men. The process is described as follows:

> A workman dips a gathering iron into the molten metal contained in one of the pots and withdraws on its extremity a ball of white hot, semi-fluid glass, which he deftly swings round to a mould close at hand. As the melted material flows into the mould a workman snips off with a pair of scissors the exact quantity, and neither more nor less, required for his tumbler-glass or dish, and brings down upon the mould the plunger of a press fixed above it. This squeezes the metal into every crevice of the mould, which is at once opened showing the tumbler, let us say, perfectly formed, but half cooled and dull in surface from contact with the surface of the plunger. The glass is picked up on the end of a forked rod by a lad and is placed for a few seconds in the intense heat of a furnace, by which means a brilliant surface is given it. But it is slightly

> warped in shape by the heat, and it is necessary to touch it again with a working tool. Thus the boy brings it to a workman who refits it upon a mould and finishes it. The glass is then carried by the youth to an annealing oven or 'lear', where, with scores of dozens more of its kind, it is gradually drawn on trays through a series of chambers, each of which is of decreasing heat, until it is landed in a cooled state at the further end of the oven.

It will be seen that it was basically a simple process, requiring little skilled labour and men could be trained to do the work in a comparatively short time. More skill was required in the design and making of the moulds and a great deal of research went into improving the moulds, both mechanically and artistically. An excellent account of the problems and the methods used to solve them is given in an article on pressed glassware in the *Pottery Gazette* (February 1886).

Because it was the cheaper end of the trade, very little is known about the designers and mould makers for pressed glass. In an article in the *Pottery Gazette* (1 August 1888), this point is stressed: 'Truly pressed glass makers have never had the credit for their productions for which they are entitled. Probably, had the pressed glass trade been recognised as it should have been, its inventors and designers would have ranked with such names as Wedgwood and Minton, but it must rest with another generation to do justice to the production of artistic pressed glass'. Indeed, it is only in recent years that pressed glass has been considered in its own right, not merely as the poor relation to cut and engraved glass, and hitherto this interest has been largely focused on the United States.

According to the *Pottery Gazette* (July 1878) the pressed-glass trade in England began about 1836, although as early as 1831 Apsley Pellatt took out a patent for a new method of assembling moulds in which he illustrated the 'machine for pressing glass by the mode lately introduced from America'. Pellatt himself, however, does not appear to have made extensive use of his patent and the early British developments seem to have taken place mostly in the Midlands, in Birmingham, Dudley and Stourbridge. Few documented English pieces of the 1830s have survived but the pressed-glass plates illustrated in Plates 123, 124, which bear the initials 'W R' were almost certainly made by the firm of Webb & Richardson of Wordsley

122 Pillar-moulded decanter and stopper, the neck and shoulder decorated by cutting. *c*. 1840. h. 12 in. *Private collection*.

during the partnership of Thomas Webb & Benjamin & W. H. Richardson which lasted from 1825 to 1840. Early pressed glass was undoubtedly made by Richardson's and by Wheeley & Davis (later Davis, Greathead & Green) of Stourbridge. Other pressed-glass saucers commemorating the Coronation of Queen Victoria in 1837 and her marriage to Albert in 1840, and some with purely ornamental patterns are possibly of Stourbridge manufacture. These saucers, and the Webb-Richardson plates, are decorated in a style that is similar to the 'lacy' patterns of the American pressed glass of the 1830s and early 1840s, that is, freely drawn relief patterns with a ground of finely stippled dots. Similar patterns were produced in France, Belgium and Sweden at the same period.

Most of the English pressed glass of the 1840s, however, sought to imitate the current styles of cut glass – often with the slight time-lag that is to be expected with imitative goods. This conscious imitation was hardly surprising considering the long indigenous tradition of glass-cutting in Britain. Cut glass was inherently expensive and few could afford it and pressed glass, which was infinitely cheaper, would obviously have a wide appeal as a close approximation of a luxury product. As the *Pottery Gazette* pointed out in an article in 1885 (1 August p. 903), the discovery of pressed glass 'gives every householder a glass where he had a tin can or a cup; it added a domestic luxury to every poor home, however humble'.

Until the introduction of the Patent Office Design Registry in 1839, we have little documentary evidence for the appearance of early pressed glass. The first registration for pressed glass, by the Birmingham firm of Rice Harris, appears in Volume 1 of *Representations* and is dated 24 January 1840. This drawing, of three goblets decorated with six broad flutes alternating with six splits, is numbered 226 and is described as follows: 'My designs are shown in the accompanying drawing applied to that description of drinking glasses manufactured by the process known by the name pressing and consist in the application of such designs in flutes (flat or hollow) and slits alternately placed, to goblets, ales, glasses and sham drams, or wine glasses above'. The second registration by Rice Harris (no. 243) appeared a few days later, on 30 January 1840. This applied to a design of six broad flutes, 'either flat, hollowed or shelled', and was applied to goblets, tumblers, ale, wine or sham dram, jelly and custard glasses.' According to the *Pottery Gazette* (1 August 1885,

123 Pressed glass plate with initials 'WR' in the pattern. Made by Webb Richardson, Stourbridge. *c.* 1836. diam. $7^1/_2$ in. *Victoria & Albert Museum.*

124 Pressed glass plate with initials 'WR' made to commemorate the coronation of Queen Victoria. Made by Webb Richardson, Stourbridge. *c.* 1837. diam. 5 in. *Private collection.*

125 Press-moulded tumbler with inscription 'GLC 1844'. h. 4 in. *Private collection.*

126 Pressed glass comport or fruit dish. Probably made by George Bacchus & Sons, Union Glass Works, Birmingham. *c.* 1850 h. $7^1/_4$ in. *Victoria & Albert Museum.*

p. 903) this was the first pressed glass tumbler to be produced, described by the writer as being exactly like 'Sowerby's no. 286 [a squat tumbler with eight flutes] but, of course, heavier and clumsier in every way and it sold at about 6s. a dozen'. Credit for this first pressed-glass tumbler, said by the writer to have been produced in 1834 or 1836, that is, several years before it was registered, is given to Rice Harris, the mould being made by James Stevens, a die sinker by trade who then had premises at Camden Street, Birmingham, and later at Bull's Head Court, Pope Street. Previously, James Stevens had made some moulds for pressed glass salts for an American glass manufacturer visiting Birmingham and he had also made moulds for salts, sugars, creams, etc. for Rice Harris. He was a man of considerable ingenuity and invention and the mould he made for the first slip-out pressed tumbler was kept by him for some time before Harris could be persuaded to try it out, considering the idea useless and impracticable. At that time pressed glass was made only in thick topped goods such as salts, sweetmeat dishes and bowls, and the difficulty of pressing up glass thin at the top was considered so impracticable as to preclude the possibility of ever adapting this process to pressing tumblers or drinking glasses, as the molten glass chilled at the top before it pressed up. However, James Stevens's invention proved practical and 'the thing once done, everybody could do it' and before long tumblers provided a considerable proportion of the output of most of the pressed-glass manufacturers. Stevens was assisted by his two sons, James and William, who later became Managers of the mould department at Sowerby's Ellison Glass Works.

The second design for tumblers produced by Stevens was said to be one of six flutes alternating with splits, the same design as Rice Harris's first registration, but registered separately by him as no. 249 on 5 February 1840.

The next registrations for pressed glass, in February and March 1840, came from another Birmingham firm, John Gold. These were for three sugar basins, one with concave sides decorated with circular motifs imitating cut hollows or printies, another with flutes and

127 Pressed glass jug and two sugar bowls registered by Sherwood & Company, Eccleston Flint Glass Works, St Helens, Lancashire, in February and May 1850. h. 4½ in. and 3½ in. *Private Collection.*

128 Pressed glass celery vase with the outer surface partly roughened. Made by James Derbyshire, Hulme, Manchester, and registered 14 May 1865. h. $10^{3}/_{4}$ in. *Private collection.*

the third with Gothic arches with fan scallops at the top. Indeed, it seems clear that the majority of patterns in pressed glass imitated the cut patterns of the 1830s and early 1840s, being mostly in the broad flute style with an increasing use of large mitre cut motifs towards the middle of the century.

By the late 1840s pressed glass was being made in considerable quantities and featured prominently at the Birmingham Exhibition of 1849 among the exhibits of Rice Harris, George Bacchus & Sons and Lloyd & Summerfield. A number of illustrations can be found in the *Journal of Design and Manufactures* and in the *Art Journal* in the late 1840s and 1850s. The fruit dish shown in Plate 126 is a good example of pressed glass imitating cutting in a slightly exaggerated and somewhat coarser form. It is very close in style to a fruit dish made by George Bacchus, illustrated in the *Journal of Design* (1850, p. 94) and was probably made by that firm. By this time the pressed-glass industry had spread to Lancashire, including Warrington, St Helens and the Manchester area. Among the earliest Lancashire registrations for pressed glass are the two sugar basins and cream jug by Sherwood & Company, Eccleston Flint Glass Works, St Helens, registered in April 1850 and illustrated in Plate 127. These, like the earlier Birmingham designs, were designed as cheaper imitations of current cut diamond patterns. Other Lancashire firms included

129 Pressed glass comport and sugar bowl registered by Percival Vickers & Co., Manchester, 6 March 1868. The under surface is partly roughened. h. 4¼ in. *Private collection.*

130 Sugar bowl of pressed glass registered by Henry Greener, Wear Flint Glass Works, Sunderland, 31 July 1869, to commemorate Gladstone's first administration. Lettered 'GLADSTONE FOR THE MILLION'. h. $4\frac{5}{8}$ in. *Private collection.*

131 Pressed glass plate commemorating the American philanthropist George Peabody (1795–1869). Made by Henry Greener, Wear Flint Glass Works, Sunderland, and registered 7 December 1869. diam. $7\frac{3}{4}$ in. *Museum & Art Gallery, Sunderland.*

132 Pressed glass plate registered by Henry Greener, Wear Flint Glass Works, Sunderland, in 1869. diam 8 in. *Private collection.*

Robinson & Bolton of Warrington; Alderton Higginbottom & Company, also of Warrington; Molineaux Webb; Percival Yates & Vickers (later Percival Vickers & Co.); and James Derbyshire & Brothers, all of whom operated in the Manchester area.

In the third quarter of the nineteenth century, the development of engraving made cut glass less fashionable and the successful imitation of cut patterns by pressing no doubt contributed to its decline, and in turn encouraged the pressed-glass manufacturers to evolve more original, less derivative styles. In the 1860s the Manchester firms evolved a whole series of dignified, restrained designs which used a roughened surface to set off simple, intaglio patterns of a formal character.

Although the inspiration was probably the delicately engraved patterns of classical ornament and vertical stripes much employed by the London firms of Apsley Pellatt and Co. and James Powell & Sons and by some of the Stourbridge firms, the pressed-glass technique produced designs that were bolder and more vigorous, giving little hint of their derivation. Molineaux Webb of Manchester in 1864 and 1865 produced a number of designs with the Greek key pattern with the outer surface partly roughened or obscured. A similar, somewhat coarser version is shown in the celery vase (Plate 128) by James Derbyshire registered on 14 May 1865. Other formal patterns consisted of concentric bands of roughened glass alternating with large raised dots of beads, or alternating stripes of clear and obscured glass. Another variant was single stars set against a roughened ground or formal leaf patterns, as in the sugar basin and comport by Percival Vickers & Company of Manchester illustrated in Plate 129.

These formal patterns were applied to a whole series of table glass – matching sugars and creams, butter dishes, plates and dishes of varying size, comports, salad bowls, celery vases and other items.

In the late 1850s press-moulding was added to the existing glass industries in the north-east, in the Newcastle, Gateshead and Sunderland area, an area which was by the late 1870s to become the most important in this field. The credit for the introduction of press-moulding to this area is given to John Neville (d. 14 January 1883), who served his apprenticeship with Bacchus & Green (known as George Bacchus & Sons from 1840) at Birmingham. Neville joined in partnership with John Sowerby at Gateshead about

1857 and set up on his own as the Neville Glass Works in 1874. The works were burnt down on 1 January 1880 but they had already been idle for about three months before the fire and in 1881 the patterns and moulds were acquired by George Davidson & Company.

The earliest registrations for pressed glass in the north-east, however, emanated from the firm of Angus & Greener of the Wear Flint Glass Works, Sunderland. Little is known about John Angus, but Henry Greener (1820–82) was born at Deptford, near Sunderland. His father was a glass engraver at the flint glass works of Messrs Vent, White & Tuer at Deptford, and his mother was the daughter of Robert Elliott, a flint-glass maker of considerable repute. It was therefore natural that he should enter the glass trade, which he did at the age of twelve, being apprenticed to John Price, glass manufacturers at Pipewell, Gateshead. By the age of nineteen he was appointed traveller for the firm but subsequently left Price's employment to work for John Sowerby at Gateshead. In 1858 he returned to Sunderland and set up in partnership with John Angus. In 1869, following the death of John Angus, the firm's name changed to Henry Greener. When Henry Greener died in 1882, the business was carried on by his son Edwin.

133 Pressed glass dish with electro-plated stand. The dish is marked 'PATENTED AUGUST 31 1875' and no. 298609 with diamond registration mark indicates that it was made by William Ford, trading under the name of John Ford, Holyrood Glass Works, Edinburgh, and registered 25 February 1876. The stand was made by William Padley & Sons, Sheffield. l. 7½ in. *Private collection.*

The earliest registration by Angus & Greener, dated December 1858, was a press-moulded dish with a star bottom and hollows round the side, very similar to the contemporary productions of the Midland and Lancashire firms. In July 1869, Henry Greener registered a design which set a fashion for commemorative glass which persisted throughout the century. This was a design applied to plates, saucers, sugars and creams, which incorporated the words 'GLADSTONE FOR THE MILLION', the letters being decorated with raised dots. This was followed in December 1869 with a similar design commemorating George Peabody and another, in November 1870, inscribed 'WILHELM FRIEDRICH'. The background of small raised dots or a fine check diaper (which recalled the 'lacy' patterns of the 1830s) was much employed by Greener from the late 1860s to the 1880s, particularly for baskets and plates.

The largest glass-works in the north-east was that of Sowerby & Company's Ellison Glass Works in East Street, Gateshead. The firm was founded by John Sowerby in 1765 at Pipewell Gate, Gateshead and was carried on by his son, John George Sowerby, who manufactured table glass, including cut and engraved glass. The Ellison

134 Pressed glass paperweights with abraded surface made by John Derbyshire, Manchester, marked with JD and an anchor and diamond registration mark for July 1874. Described as a 'lion after Landseer'. h. $4^3/_4$ in. *Victoria & Albert Museum.*

works were started about 1838 and when John Neville joined the firm in 1857 it was known as Sowerby & Neville. It was presumably at about that time that the manufacture of pressed glass was introduced. Little is known about their early productions in pressed glass as it was not until 1872 that Sowerby & Company registered their designs. The first registrations, in February 1872, included a covered butter dish, with gadrooning and a classical handle, which seems to be derived from a silver shape; a decanter with bands imitating diamond-cutting and with panels of leaf ornament recalling the patterns of Molineaux Webb and other Manchester firms in the mid-1860s. The first extant pattern book of Sowerby & Company includes these registrations and several other designs with leaf ornament against an obscured ground. It also includes a service (no. 990) with a running band of oak leaves and acorns made in both obscured and bright glass. A number of the designs, notably those for sugar basins, carafes and ups, goblets and tumblers, are in the styles current in pressed glass in the mid-1850s and it is probable that the moulds date from that period. The range of goods is extensive for, apart from complete services, the catalogue illustrates every conceivable item of domestic glassware from egg cups to cheese stands, ink bottles and tobacco jars and even such an exotic item as an opium lamp. By 1880 the works occupied an area a quarter of a mile square and eight furnaces were in operation.

Apart from Sowerby's, one of the most important pressed-glass works in the north-east was that of George Davidson & Company, Teams Glass Works, Gateshead. George Davidson, the son of a miller, was born at Cow Close Hill, near Ravensworth Castle, on 29 September 1822. He left school at an early age and entered the building trade, which he abandoned after a number of years to become a butcher. It was not until 1867 or 1868, when he was a prominent citizen and a member of the town council, that he set up the Teams Glass Works, starting in a small way with only a handful of men. By the 1880s, under the management of his son Thomas (1860–1937), it had become one of the leading firms in the area, employing three hundred and fifty men in 1886, with a monthly output of two hundred to two hundred and fifty tons of pressed glass. In 1891 the control of the firm passed to Thomas Davidson, who designed ninety per cent of the firm's domestic goods.

The earliest Davidson registrations appear to have been made in

135 Pressed glass ornament in the form of a coal truck registered by W. H. Heppell, Newcastle on Tyne, in 1880. h. $3^1/_2$ in. *Victoria & Albert Museum.*

January and February 1877. These were for two urn-shaped vases in classical style, very similar to those being produced by other firms about the same time. The classical style featured prominently in the 1870s, both in the registrations of various Manchester firms as well as in those emanating from the north-east. In December 1872, J. J. & T. Derbyshire of Manchester produced a glass breakfast set in a simple classical design, and an urn-shaped celery vase with classical motifs. In January 1873, Ker, Webb & Co., also of Manchester, registered a tobacco jar of classical form. A deep purple slag glass spill vase which appears to be almost jet black, was registered by John Derbyshire in April 1876, and a number of similar classical designs were registered by Sowerby between 1876 and 1878, including some designs derived from silver shapes in the 'Adam' style, together with a candlestick in the form of a Corinthian column.

A particularly interesting development in the 1870s and early 1880s was the press-moulding of glass in three-dimensional, imitative forms. Moulded glass had been used for small sculptures in the mid-century, as in the busts of Queen Victoria and Prince Albert, made by both F. & C. Osler and Lloyd and Summerfield of Birmingham. In the mid-1860s John Ford of the Holyrood Glass Works, Edinburgh had produced a pair of tazzas with caryatid figures of a fisher boy and girl and in 1866 Robinson & Bolton of Warrington had registered a tumbler in the form of a barrel, but it was not until the 1870s that pressed glass became a popular medium for novelties of this sort. The fashion was an international one, and there are indications that the British fashion was related to that in the United States. The imitative form was, as in the case of the John Ford tazzas, sometimes used merely for part of the vessel, as in the dolphin stems registered by Percival Vickers and Molineaux Webb in 1874 and 1875, and in a Sowerby dish of 1875 with handles in the form of monkeys, but most of the imitative forms represented the whole of the vessel. One of the most popular was a swan, first registered by Hodgetts, Richardson & Son in 1872, and later taken up by many firms. An even more popular item was a dismembered hand, first registered by Burtles Tate & Company, of Manchester and Bolton, in October 1871, as a chimney piece ornament. A similar upright hand was registered by J. J. & T. Derbyshire in May of the following year. In 1874, Derbyshire registered the variant of a hand supporting a vase, in this instance composed of leaves and bulrushes. The hand holding a vase was probably the most popular form and was widely produced not only in Britain but throughout Europe and the United States. A large number of extant examples, particularly those in opaque white or opalescent glass with enamelled decoration, are undoubtedly of Bohemian origin.

A severed hand lying on an oval base was registered by Edward Bolton of Warrington in October 1874, and a dish formed of a pair of hands lying side by side with the wrists covered by vine leaves and grapes, was registered by John Ford of the Holyrood Glassworks, Edinburgh, in February 1876 (Plate 133). An identical design had already been patented in the United States by W. L. Libbey & Sons in the previous year and it is probable that the two firms were acting under an arrangement.

The severed hand by Edward Bolton was probably intended as a

136 Sugar basin of opaque white pressed glass. On one side, a portrait head of Benjamin Disraeli, Earl of Beaconsfield, and on the other an inscription 'Earl Beaconsfield, the Hero of the Congress, Berlin, July 1878'. Registered by Henry Greener, Wear Flint Glass Works, Sunderland, 31 August 1878. h. $5^1/_2$ in. *Private collection.*

137 Pressed glass plate commemorating John Bright (1811–89) and his fight for the repeal of the Corn Law in the 1840s. diam 5 in. *Private collection.*

138 Pressed glass plate with 'A PRESENT FROM THE ISLE OF MAN' and an engraved inscription 'Mrs. Anderson 1894'. Made by Sowerby's Ellison Glass Works, Gateshead on Tyne. diam. $8^{7}/_{8}$ in. *Private collection.*

paperweight and many of the three-dimensional, imitative pieces were conceived for this purpose. In July 1874, John Derbyshire produced a 'lion after Landseer' (Plate 134). Although registered as a paperweight, these lions, which were made in various sizes, are often found in pairs and were evidently used as chimneypiece ornaments in the manner of Staffordshire pottery dogs. In September 1874 Derbyshire produced a 'Britannia' paperweight and a 'Sphinx' paperweight in July 1875. This was countered by Molineaux Webb with a 'Winged Sphinx' in May 1876. John Derbyshire also produced both a 'Punch' and a 'Judy' paperweight about 1875.

Innumerable other novelties, intended either as spill holders, ornaments or small flower holders, included a lady's boot, registered by John Derbyshire in 1875 and later produced by a number of firms, including Sowerby's; a coal wagon (Plate 135); a wheelbarrow registered by W. H. Heppell in 1880; a miniature cradle registered by the same firm in 1881; and various glass boats, which have already been described in the chapter on 'Centrepieces and Flower Stands'.

139 Pressed glass plate and bowl commemorating Queen Victoria's Jubilee of 1887: *Left* Probably made by George Davidson, Gateshead. diam. 10 in. *Right* Made by Matthew Turnbull, Sunderland. diam. $7\frac{1}{2}$ in. *Private collection.*

Some of the most attractive pressed glass of the late 1870s and 1880s was in Sowerby's 'Patent Queen's Ivory Ware', introduced in 1879. The opaque body, indeed, has a similar appearance to cream-coloured earthenware, which was called 'Queen's Ware' by Wedgwood in the eighteenth century. Sowerby's product is described by the *Pottery Gazette* (January 1880) as being 'in entirely new designs corresponding with carved ivory. It is also being made from original models by eminent artists – jardinieres, rose baskets, table decorations, vases, specimen vases, toilet table requisites, dessert ware, teacups and saucers, tiles for cabinet work and stoves, card trays, etc'. Twenty examples of this 'Patent Queen's Ivory Ware', including the large bowl shown in Plate 147 were illustrated in the supplement to the *Pottery Gazette* (1 November 1879). They include several examples with Japanese motifs, a 'Jack and Jill' vase, two

140 Pressed glass plate made to commemorate the Golden Jubilee of Queen Victoria in 1887 by Sowerby's Ellison Glass Works, Gateshead on Tyne. diam. 9⅞ in. *Victoria & Albert Museum.*

swan vases, several baskets and a candlestick in classical style. Other designs followed including many in a Japanese style, more nursery rhyme subjects, many designs imitating basket work, simple daisy (Plate 148) and sunflower patterns, a parrot design and two with peacocks (Plate 149). Practically all of them can be termed 'aesthetic' and it is significant that Sowerby's had chosen an 'aesthetic' motif, the peacock's head, as their trade-mark, which they registered on 12 July 1876. Unfortunately, it has not been possible to ascertain which artists were responsible for these designs but some of them may have been designed by John G. Sowerby who was well known as an illustrator of children's books in a style that had considerable affinity with the work of Kate Greenaway and Walter Crane. He was also a landscape painter of some ability and a prominent member of the Newcastle Arts Association and it was therefore quite natural

141 Pressed glass bowl commemorating the Silver Wedding Anniversary of the Prince and Princess of Wales in 1888. Made by Henry Greener, Wear Flint Glass Works, Sunderland, and registered in that year. w. $9^1/_2$ in. *Private collection.*

that he should introduce the 'aesthetic' style into the products of the family firm.

Apart from the 'Patent Queen's Ivory Ware', Sowerby's also produced an opaque glass which they called 'Vitro-Porcelain' in a wide variety of colours, the same designs being used for the different varieties, and for flint and opalescent glass. The plain colours included turquoise, a soft olive green, gold and white, the latter being known as 'Blanc de Lait', and black, known as 'Jet'. Motifs such as individual flowers were sometimes painted in colours or gilt. The marbled colours included Green Malachite, Brown Malachite, Tortoiseshell Ware, a purple slag glass, and various other effects including a deep turquoise with splodges of opaque white. In the marbled glass, the finely modelled detail and the crispness of the design is often lost.

The numerous items produced by Sowerby in the 'aesthetic' style are among the most attractive pieces of pressed glass produced in this country and are now eagerly sought by collectors. Reviewing Sowerby's exhibit at the International Health Exhibition of 1884, the *Pottery Gazette* remarks that 'their fancy glass should have been in the art gallery, but being of such a cheap and popular character, we suppose they were inadmissible. Still in taste and aesthetic treatment they rank as art goods, notwithstanding their cheapness. We may call it "Art for the million"'.

Similar opaque and slag glass was produced by other firms in the north-east, notably by W. H. Heppell, Greener & Co., and George Davidson, but none of it was in the 'aesthetic' taste favoured by Sowerby. Some of the Davidson glass, however, was equally attractive, notably several designs with roses, thistles and shamrocks, and several designs with branches of coral and shells. Heppell's were responsible for a number of eccentric designs, including a grotesque fish vase and a sugar basin and jug in the form of a helmet and visor. These designs, together with the rest of the moulds, were taken over by George Davidson in 1884 when the firm of W. H. Heppell was dissolved.

Some of the most interesting pressed glass of the nineteenth century was made for commemorative purposes, most of it emanating from the north-east. A considerable body of the glass was made to celebrate various royal occasions. The early pressed glass saucers commemorating the Coronation and marriage of Queen Victoria

142 Water set consisting of a jug, two tumblers and a tray in 'Pearline' glass, registered by George Davidson, Gateshead, and illustrated in the *Pottery Gazette* as part of their '1889 Suite'. *Victoria & Albert Museum.*

143 Pressed glass salad bowl made by Sowerby's Ellison Glass Works, Gateshead, and illustrated in the firm's catalogue of *c.* 1888 pattern no. 1913. diam. 10 in. *Private collection.*

144 Pressed glass celery vase made by George Davidson & Co., Gateshead on Tyne. *c.* 1885. Marked with the firm's lion crest trademark. h. $9^1/_4$ in. *Victoria & Albert Museum.*

have already been discussed. The 1887 Jubilee was commemorated by many firms. The *Pottery Gazette* (1 March 1887) commented on this in these terms; 'Glass manufacturers have not been behind those in other trades in the production of what are called Jubilee Goods, and I only hope none of the firms will find they have burnt their fingers. Such an immense number of Jubilee articles have been put on the market that I am afraid the public appetite will be more than satisfied.'

The Sowerby contribution was a pressed-glass plate and bowl with a medallion portrait of the Queen (Plate 140) – described by the *Pottery Gazette* as 'really a likeness' – but most firms issued designs incorporating the words 'The Queen's Jubilee' or 'Queen Victoria's Jubilee', the dates 1837 and 1887, with a crown and other devices. The plate and bowl illustrated in Plate 139 are typical examples with the lettering composed of raised dots, in the manner introduced by Greener in 1869 (Plates 130, 131). Sugars and creams were also issued with similar designs. Similar designs were issued for the 1897 Jubilee and this practice has continued for many royal occasions, even up to the present day.

The Silver Wedding Anniversary of the Prince and Princess of Wales on 10 March 1888, was marked by a number of firms including

145 Mould-blown decanter and stopper registered by Edward Moore & Co., Tyne Flint Glass Works, South Shields, 29 June 1861. *Private collection.*

Greener & Co. (Plate 141) and George Davidson. The visit of H.R.H. Princess Louise and the Marquis of Lorne to Halifax, Nova Scotia, in November 1878 was commemorated by Greener with a design including medallion portraits which appeared on sugar basins, jugs, butter dishes, plates and spoonholders, in flint glass and in opaque glass in shades of opal, blue, malachite and black.

Prominent statesmen were similarly celebrated by the glass manufacturers. A saucer by an unknown manufacturer commemorated John Bright (1811–89) and his fight for the Repeal of the Corn Laws in the 1840s (Plate 137). Gladstone's first administration of 1868–74 was commemorated by Henry Greener. Benjamin Disraeli, who became Earl Beaconsfield on 16 August 1876, received a more sophisticated tribute, also by Greener, in the form of an opaque white sugar basin and jug issued to mark his success at the Berlin Congress of 1878 on the Eastern Question (Plate 136). Lesser mortals such as the oarsman Edward Hanlon (Champion of the World November 15th 1880 who beat Tricket of NSW) were also commemorated, in this case by a pressed-glass mug made by Henry Greener of the Wear Flint Glass Works, Sunderland. The manufacturer of a plate commemorating the opening of the Forth Bridge on 4 March 1890 is not known but another piece with a Scottish appeal is the Robert Burns bowl registered by Sowerby in 1888. The Isle of Man plate (Plate 138), similarly, does not commemorate any particular event but was issued as a holiday souvenir which could be engraved with the name of the purchaser. Similar pressed-glass plates were produced for the Christmas trade with wreaths of holly and the words 'The Compliment of the Season' in the familiar lettering composed of raised dots.

Owing to the expense of producing moulds, patterns could remain in use for twenty years or more and as various firms went out of production, their moulds were taken over by other firms. In spite of this, new patterns were continually being introduced.

In the 1880s the revival of glass-cutting led the pressed-glass manufacturers to a renewed imitation of cut glass styles. The 1880s and 1890s was the period of the so-called 'Brilliant' cut glass, not only in England but throughout Europe and the United States, and these 'Brilliant' patterns were successfully imitated in pressed glass. The so-called 'Hobnail' pattern was popular with many firms, notably with Percival Vickers & Co., who registered two such patterns

146 Pressed glass two-handled bowl and cut-glass silver-mounted bowl in the 'Queen Anne' style. *Left* Registered by Edward Moore & Co., South Shields, in 1887. *Right* Registered by John Walsh Walsh, Soho & Vesta Glass Works, Birmingham, in 1884. h. 4 in. and $3^1/_2$ in. *Private collections.*

147 Pressed glass bowl of Sowerby's 'Patent Queen's Ware' registered by the firm on 6 June 1879. *Victoria & Albert Museum.*

in 1884 and 1885, and George Davidson who issued a Hobnail Suite in November 1885. Molineaux Webb produced a similar pattern in July 1888, which they called 'The Duchess Suite'. Greener's produced several star patterns, including the 'Royal Star' pattern, a diamond-cut star encircled by smaller stars of a different shape, in 1887. These patterns were in their turn imitated by other firms often with only slight variations.

These 'Brilliant' patterns were often set in panels divided by heavy ribs of glass. George Davidson produced both an '1889' and an '1890' suite in this manner. These were made in their patent 'Blue Pearline' as well as in clear glass. This 'Blue Pearline', registered in 1889, was made in a deep turquoise blue which shaded to a pale, opaque turquoise in the thicker parts of the glass. The articles were press-moulded in the usual way, then allowed to cool slightly, and then reheated. The reheated portions struck a paler opalescent colour of the shade of the body colour or an opalescent white. It was, therefore, particularly suitable for designs incorporating ribs or pillars which stood out in the pearly opaque pale blue, contrasting with the deeper clear turquoise of the thinner parts which were usually decorated with small diamond patterns imitating cutting

148 Pressed glass plate of Sowerby's 'Patent Queen's Ware' registered by the firm on 30 August 1878. diam. 9 in. *Ulster Museum.*

(Plate 142). The thicker portion at the top, and the fan scallops were also pale and opaque. These designs were also made in a greenish yellow glass (now known as 'vaseline'), which was also opaque and pale in the thicker parts. Similar patterns with fan scallops and fine diamond or star patterns were produced by Sowerby (Plate 143) but only in flint glass.

One suite of Davidson's 'Blue Pearline' (no. 643), registered in October 1890, had a design composed entirely of ribs or pillars. The suite included a water set, sugar and cream, salad bowl, celery, butter dish, biscuit barrel and various sizes of jugs and dishes. The bases were embellished with a Vandyke star. Ribbed or pillared patterns such as these were common throughout the late 1880s and 1890s. Pillared dishes were produced by Sowerby's in 1887 and a set of pillared dishes by Edward Bolton of Warrington was registered in 1888. These 'pillars' or 'gadroons' may partly be regarded as a harking back to the 1840s, but they also owed something to earlier silver styles. Curved gadroons, in the manner of early eighteenth-century silver, were used by several manufacturers to produce various articles in the so-called 'Queen Anne' style. The pressed-glass sugar basin by Edward Moore of South Shields and the silver-

149 Pressed glass dish in the cream colour known as 'Patent Queen's Ware'. Impressed decoration of peacocks and sunflowers around the border and peacock feathers in the central sunken part. Underside has patent office mark for 8 February 1879. *Victoria & Albert Museum.*

mounted cut-glass bowl by John Walsh Walsh of Birmingham, shown in Plate 146 are typical examples. Other silver styles, notably the 'Adam' style, were imitated in pressed glass, particularly for items such as biscuit barrels, sauceboat-shaped sugar basins, cream jugs and candlesticks.

A number of the heavy cut patterns of the late 1840s and 1850s were reflected in the pressed glass of the 1880s. Some of these designs have a somewhat fortuitous resemblance to art nouveau as the imitative mitre cuts are arranged in swirling or assymetrical patterns. The celery vase by George Davidson (Plate 144) is a typical example which superficially seems to have the sinuous curves of art nouveau but is in fact a revival of a mid-century pattern and has an almost exact counterpart in a cut-glass dish made by Richardson's about 1848. The heavy cut patterns of the mid-century had in fact been revived earlier by Sowerby's, about 1874, in three pressed glass services which they entitled 'Diamonds and Prisms', 'Prisms' and 'Diamonds'. The first pattern combined imitative prismatic cutting arranged in fan shapes with horizontal rows of diamonds in between, the general effect being rather heavy and clumsy. The service or suite comprised carafe and up, salad bowl, covered sugar, decanter, celery, a centrepiece formed from a bowl and an upturned celery, a butter dish, two salts, bowls, dishes, plates and a tumbler. The 'Prisms' service was much simpler and more restrained and the 'Diamond' service was almost Georgian in conception with an all-over diamond diaper.

CHAPTER 12

LATER FANCY GLASS

AN INCREDIBLE variety of fancy glass was produced, notably in the Stourbridge area and in Birmingham, during the last twenty-five years of Victoria's reign. The *Pottery Gazette* from 1877 to 1901 lists hundreds of different novelties, many of which cannot now be positively identified, as they are merely mentioned by name and not precisely described, and in few cases are they illustrated. The situation is also confused because many varieties of fancy glass have, in recent years, been given names which are only dealers' terms, used for convenience, and which bear no relation to the contemporary, somewhat ephemeral name, given to the glass at the time of manufacture. However, some of the fancy glass can be precisely identified through registration in the Patent Office Design Registers, by contemporary trade catalogues such as those of Silber and Fleming, merchants and importers, of 56 Wood Street, London, or by extant records in the archives of surviving firms. Marked and signed pieces, particularly by leading manufacturers such as Stevens & Williams and Thomas Webb, can be found in the collections at Stourbridge, Brierley Hill, and elsewhere.

A distinctive category of fancy glass is iridescent glass, which was not produced by British manufacturers until the late 1870s. At the London International Exhibition of 1862, a Hungarian firm exhibited iridescent glass 'which when placed in indirect rays of light displayed all the brilliant colourings of a prism'. Similar glass was produced by the Austrian firm of Lobmeyer at the Vienna Exhibition of 1873 and two years later the idea was again taken up by some Bohemian manufacturers. According to the *Pottery Gazette* (October

1877, p. 69) the firm of Wittmann & Roth, of Marlborough Street, London, displayed in their showrooms a collection of iridescent glass decanters, goblets and vases, modelled on antique shapes, in the early summer of 1876. As Wittmann & Roth were dealers and importers, and not glass manufacturers, it is probable that this glass was imported, probably from Bohemia, although it is certain that by the following year it was being produced by British firms. On 29 August 1877, an application for letters patent was taken out by Thomas Webb & Sons for an improved means of producing iridescent colours on glass and the patent was finally sealed on 27 February 1878. The *Pottery Gazette* (May 1878, p. 204) describes the process as follows: 'Chloride of tin, or tin salt, is burnt in a furnace, and the glass having an affinity for it, when hot receives the fumes, and so at once an iridescent surface is produced. To give greater depth to the colour or tints, nitrate of barium and strontium is used in small proportions. By this patent, the glass is not reheated, but the iridescence is produced during the manufacture of the article when in the hands of the blower and while on the punty'. An early example of Thomas Webb's iridescent glass, which they called 'Bronze Glass', acquired by the Royal Scottish Museum, Edinburgh, in 1878, is illustrated in Plate 151. The glass was thick and heavy and with its purplish bronze iridescent surface had the appearance of oxidised steel or copper. Shapes were generally classical, following the forms of Ancient Greek or Roman vessels, although it was also produced in a variety of fancy shapes, often with applied shell feet and handles. Queen Victoria is said to have greatly admired it when she saw it exhibited at Messrs Goode's showrooms in Audley Street, considering that it would 'meet the taste of a refined public'. Indeed, this new Bronze Glass was also exhibited by the Grosvenor Gallery in New Bond Street, the veritable headquarters of the 'aesthetic' movement and was also highly prized by Mrs Loftie in *The Dining Room*, one of the volumes in the Macmillan 'Art at Home' series, published in London in 1878. The firm enjoyed a considerable success with this product at the Paris Exhibition of 1878 and in October of that year an amplification of the process gave a fine crackled effect to the glass, which was produced in green as well as bronze under the name 'Scarabeous Glass'. It was coloured to represent the natural tints of the beetle's wing and the surface was broken up into a thousand fissures to complete the imitation. This crackled

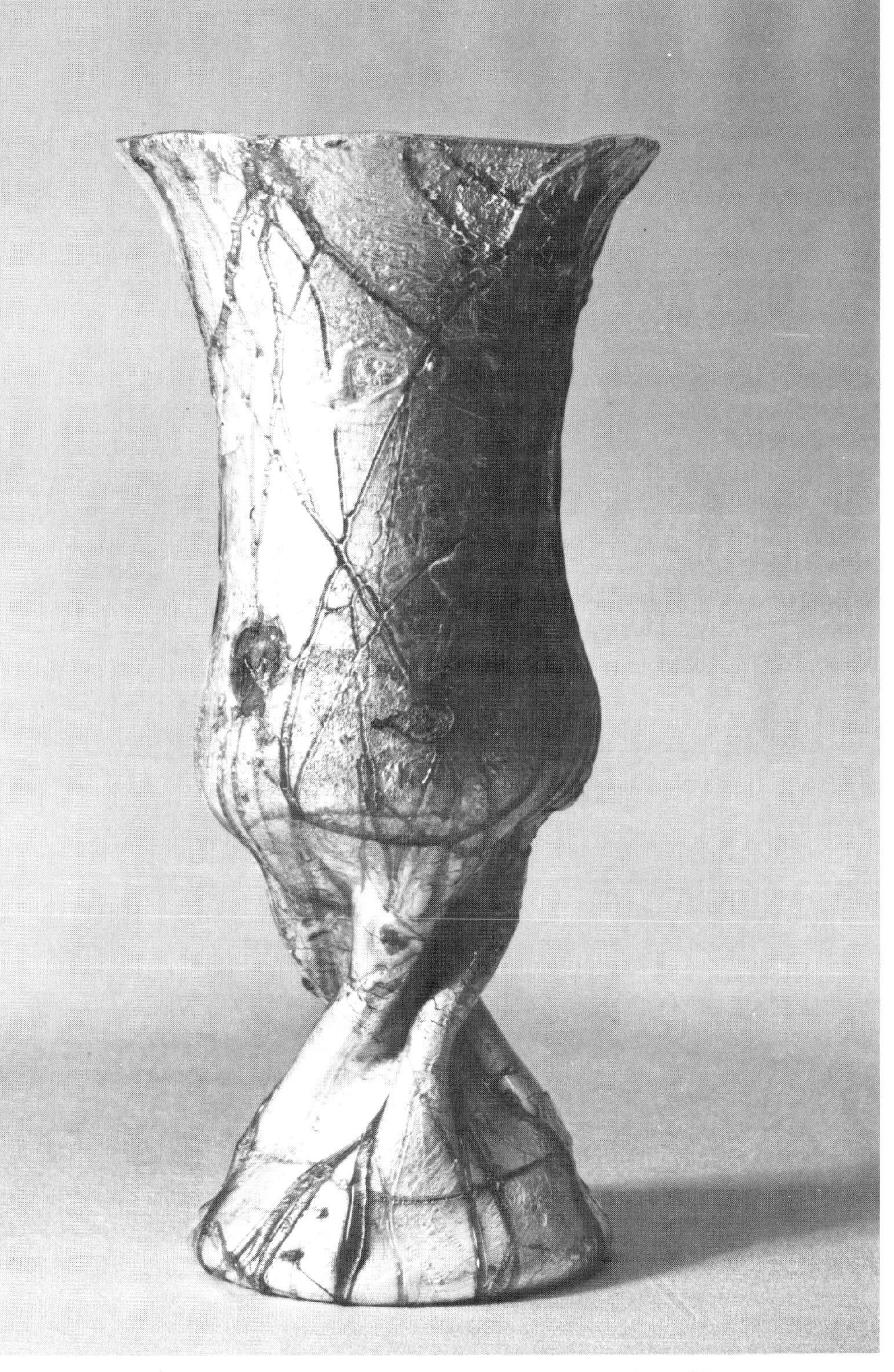

150 'Silveria' glass vase. Layered glass with enclosed silver leaf and green glass trailing. Made by Stevens & Williams, Brierley Hill. *c.* 1900. Marked 'S & W'. h. 12¾ in. *Victoria & Albert Museum.*

effect was achieved by plunging the iridescent glass into cold water while it was still hot. Although not new, this glass was much admired at the Australian Centennial Exhibition of 1888. The later examples were decorated with gilding, usually with trailing sprays of blossom.

In spite of their patent, Webb's by no means had the monopoly of the production of iridescent glass in Britain. The firm of Alexander D. Jenkinson of Norton Park, Edinburgh was also producing iridescent glass in 1877. The *Pottery Gazette* (1 June 1880) states that moulded iridescent glass was being produced by Henry Greener & Co. of Sunderland, and John Northwood shortly before joining Stevens & Williams in 1881 or 1882, produced a similar ware to Webb's Bronze Glass, of a deep green with a purple sheen.

Richardson's appear to have introduced iridescent glass for vases and centrepieces late in 1877 and early in the following year they produced a whole range of purple iridescent and bronze glass, mostly for vases. Some were in fairly simple smooth shapes with applied ribbed handles and shell prunts, others were ribbed and with indentations – described as 'Knocked in 4 times'. Others had slightly projecting spikes or pimples, or applied leaves. There was also a revival of Richardson's bronze glass in 1891. Various urn-shaped vases were produced, also some in somewhat Chinese shapes

151 Bowl of iridescent 'Bronze' glass, made by Thomas Webb & Sons, Stourbridge. 1878. h. $2^3/_4$ in. *Royal Scottish Museum, Edinburgh.*

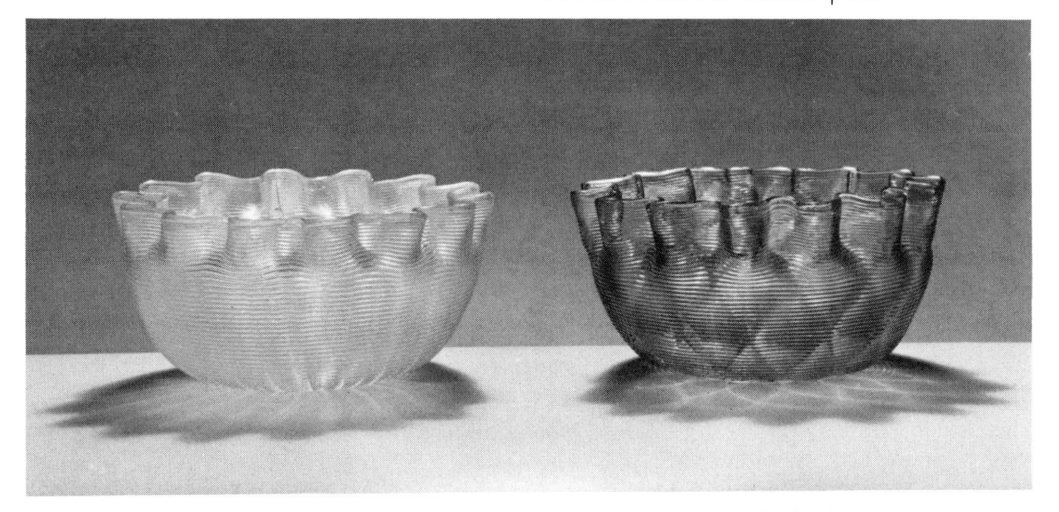

152 Two fingerbowls made by Richardson's of Stourbridge. *c.* 1882. *Left* Flint body with opalescent threads blown in a ribbed mould, with crimped top. *Right* Pale rose body with citron threads blown in diamond-patterned mould, with crimped top. Each diam. 5 in. *Private collection.*

with ring handles, others enriched with painted decoration.

The introduction of gold or silver foil between layers of clear or coloured glass resulted in several types of fancy glass produced from 1883 onwards. Among the earliest was the 'Argentine' or 'Oroide' glass produced by Edward Webb at the White House Glassworks, Wordsley and described in the *Pottery Gazette* (January 1883) and in the supplement to that journal in May of the same year. The credit for its introduction was given to the manager of the art glass department, Arthur J. Nash, who later emigrated to the United States, joining the firm of Tiffany & Co, and later, in 1919, setting up on his own with his two sons, Leslie and Douglas. The firm advertised it as being 'a reproduction of old Venetian art glass for decorative purposes', adding that 'it has all the appearance of the fragility of the old Venetian ware and the strength of English solidity'. It was called 'Argentine' when silver was introduced and 'Oroide' when gold was incorporated. The effect was obtained by introducing a film of silver or gold between two layers of glass; in some cases the layers were of the same colour, in others, contrasting, the metal foil being used to form 'graceful patterns'. Sometimes these silver or gold patterns closely approximated to the tint of the glass itself so that it was only by holding the objects in different lights that the patterns could be clearly discerned. In other instances the tint of the glass was in marked contrast to the gold or silver of the pattern. In another variety the metallic film was made to crack into innumerable minute patches and dots, resembling what was called 'oriental crackle'.

An even more elaborate version of this type of glass, known as 'Silveria' was introduced by Stevens & Williams about the turn of the century (Plate 150). A solid sheet of silver foil was trapped between two layers of clear crystal glass. In addition, streaks of coloured glass, predominantly green, but also red, yellow and other hues, were trailed over the foil in irregular, meandering designs. The glass was used for vases and dishes in the somewhat organic forms associated with the art nouveau style. The original silver lustre was retained by the exclusion of air from the foil, but occasionally a piece will be found where surface crazing has occurred in the outer layers causing oxidisation and the consequent tarnishing and discolouration of the silver.

Another luxury type of glass, produced by Stevens & Williams, involved a deposit of silver on the surface of the glass, which was subsequently engraved. This glass, which was called 'Damascened' glass, was patented in 1885. Copper was sometimes used as an

153 Two vases in clear glass, the bodies with applied threading in blue and red, with applied ribbed handles and furnace-wrought collars. Made by Richardson's of Stourbridge. *c.* 1877. *Private collection.*

154 Jug and tumbler with all-over flint threading decorated with intaglio cutting in the style known as 'Silver threading'. Probably made by Stevens & Williams, Brierley Hill. *c.* 1887. *Private collection.*

alternative to silver. The patterns were generally somewhat Oriental in style, consisting of formal arabesques, and were the work of a Frenchman named Oscar Pierre Erard. Comparatively little of this glass was made as it was too expensive to be commercially viable. Similar glass, with encrusted arabesque decoration in silver, known as '*Procède intercristal*', had been exhibited by the firm of Grichois, Paris, at the Paris Exhibition of 1855, and it is probable that Erard brought this technique from France.

Another different method of using gold with glass was evolved by the executors of the late Joseph Webb at the Coalbourn Hill Glass Works, Stourbridge, for their 'New Gold Glass' described in the *Pottery Gazette* (March 1883). This glass – 'made in various ornamental shapes for the drawing room' – had a crumpled surface, coloured with gold, which was worked into it in the process of manufacture. 'The gold surface' says the report 'is not to be compared with gilding, it being, as it were, a top layer of the glass, and is brought out in combination with different coloured bodies. Some are worked out in green and amber glass. The elevations of the crumpled shapes admit the light through which shows up the tinge, and adds to the effect'.

An important contribution to the development of certain types of fancy glass was the development of a glass threading machine which made possible the mechanical coiling of a thread, or threads of molten glass round a glass bulb or cylinder which was then blown into a mould – usually a ribbed mould. A patent for this machine was taken out by William James Hodgetts of Hodgetts, Richardson & Son in 1876. This threaded glass could be fashioned into jugs, carafes, vases, bowls and other articles in the usual way.

A further similar patent for the mechanical threading of glass was taken out the following year, in December 1877 by William Henry Stevens on behalf of Stevens & Williams.

In the late 1870s and 1880s this mechanical threading was much used for the decoration of table glass as well as for fancy articles (Plate 153), and many examples appear in the Richardson pattern book for 1877.

Engraving was often used in combination with the threading. A decanter and jug, delicately engraved with flowers and rustic twigs with turquoise threading at the base now in the Victoria & Albert Museum are also probably by Richardson's. Many other articles with mechanical threading occur in the Richardson pattern books of this period including the two finger bowls shown in Plate 152. The one on the left is of flint glass and opalescent threading blown in a ribbed mould; that on the right is of pale rose with citron threading blown in a diamond patterned mould. Richardson's also made vases with flint-threaded bodies decorated with furnace-wrought applied decoration such as flowers, leaves and raspberry prunts. This firm also made extensive use of mechanical threading for the decoration of flower stands and centrepieces, either in flint or in a variety of colours including turquoise, ruby, citron, heliotrope and opalescent.

A more expensive and sophisticated type of threaded fancy glass was the 'Tapestry' glass of Stevens & Williams, introduced in 1887. This was a triple layered flint glass, blown in a ribbed mould, with a threaded outer layer. The inner layer was painted and gilt, usually with floral patterns, often in a Persian style. The outer threaded layer gave to the pattern the effect of the horizontal ribs of a woven tapestry. This tapestry glass is said to have been designed by Erard.

Threaded glass was also decorated with intaglio work at Stevens & Williams. The articles were of flint glass threaded all over in flint – known as 'silver threading'. The intaglio patterns, usually floral, were cut through the threads, the pattern appearing clear and smooth against the threaded background (Plate 154). This type of glass was extensively used at the end of the Victorian period for silver mounted articles – claret jugs, decanters, toilet services and vases.

Considerable attention was paid in the late 1870s and 1880s to the production of an ivory bodied glass which sought to imitate the appearance of porcelain or creamware. Sowerby's 'Patent Ivory Queen's Ware' and their white 'Vitro Porcelain' are described in the chapter on pressed glass. Among the other ivory bodied glass was Thomas Webb's 'ivory' glass, first produced about 1884, and usually decorated with raised gold, silver or enamelled decoration in the workshop of Jules Barbe. Similar vases were produced by Edward Webb of Wordsley and a typical example is shown in Plate 162. An 'Ivorine' glass was also produced by Richardson's in 1884, often decorated with applied flowers, leaves and pinchings in flint. Many of these vases, like those by Thomas Webb, were decorated by gilding, mostly with sprays of blossom and leaves, butterflies,

155 Flint glass bowl with air enclosed and threaded pattern in pillar effect worked by the pull-up machine. Made by Stevens & Williams, Brierley Hill. *c.* 1885. *Borough of Stourbridge (Northwood Collection).*

dragonflies and other insects. This gilding appears to have been executed by Erard, who is better known for his work for Stevens & Williams. In 1887 Webb's introduced an 'Old Ivory' glass which was carved in designs derived from Chinese, Japanese and other historic ornament (Plate 163).

Edward Webb, of the White House Glass Works, Wordsley, produced a 'Worcester Ivory Glass' in 1883, which he claimed was a close imitation of Worcester porcelain, with edgings of turquoise, ruby pink and other colours. Edward Webb produced a further development of this in 1885 which he designated as 'Dresden Cameo'.

It is impossible to mention all the different coloured opaque bodies that were developed during the 1880s, each manufacturer claiming to have introduced a completely new colour. Among the more distinguished was Thomas Webb's '*Sanguis Dragonis*', a rich maroon red glass, introduced about 1884. At the Australian Centennial Exhibition of 1888, Webb showed handsome '*Sanguis Dragonis*' vases surmounted by gilt elephant's head handles, the body being ornamented with gilding in Indian style.

Many varieties of glass were produced under the general designation of satin glass. The basic feature was that the outer surface of the glass was given a semi-matt finish by means of acid, or sometimes by sandblasting. A further refinement was the trapping of air between the layers in moulded recesses so that the pattern showed through the outer layer. The earliest patent for this was taken out by Benjamin Richardson in 1858. A gather of glass was blown into a patterned mould which carried the pattern in projected form, resulting in a vessel with an indented surface pattern. While still in a molten state the glass was given an outer casing, the air being trapped between the two layers. Alternatively, the moulded piece was placed in a cup of glass blown to receive it, the worker then blowing and reshaping the two layers. Richardson's patent, however, did not mention a semi-matt or satin finish, and it appears that satin glass as we know it was not fully developed until the 1880s. This satin glass normally consisted of two or three layers. The inner body of the glass was generally opaque, the next layer coloured, the third layer, when present, of clear crystal glass, and the outer surface was always semi-matt (Plates 160, 161). Among the earliest named varieties of English satin glass were Boulton & Mills '*Nacre de Perle*', introduced

156 'Moss Agate' vase with crackled and colour-streaked body, made by Stevens & Williams, Brierley Hill. *c.* 1888. In the possession of the makers. h. 5¾ in. *Photograph Victoria & Albert Museum.*

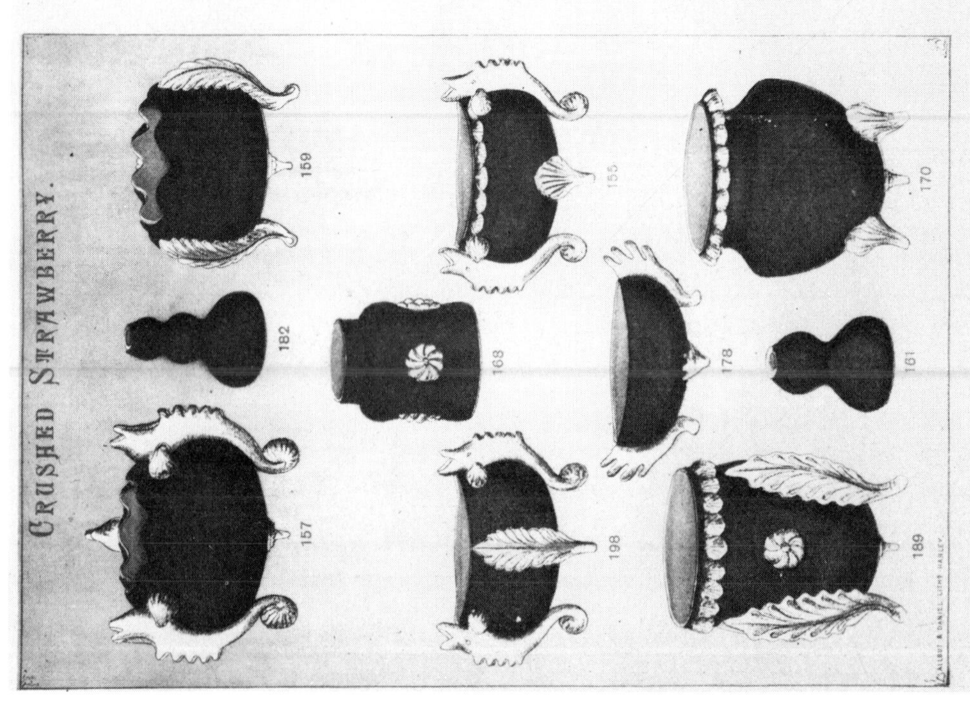

157 Advertisement from the *Pottery Gazette* for November 1883 for the 'Crushed Strawberry' and 'Electric Blue' glass by John Walsh Walsh, Soho & Vesta Glass Works, Birmingham, the bowls and vases being decorated with applied fish, pincered leaves and frills, 'raspberry' and other prunts in clear flint glass.

the Audnam Glass Works, Stourbridge, in 1885 and a similar pearl satin glass known as '*Verre-de-Soie*', developed by Frederick Carder at Stevens & Williams about 1886. Stuart & Sons of the Red House Glass Works, Stourbridge produced a *moiré* patterned satin glass with the appearance of watered silk. A similar satin glass by John Walsh Walsh of Birmingham was registered as 'Broché' glass. This was described by the *Pottery Gazette* (1 December 1886) as 'a clever imitation of satin and velvet which can be applied to almost any class or article'. In fact satin glass was mostly used for vases and ornaments although jugs, sugar basins and cream jugs and other articles are found. Satin glass was also extensively used for fairy lights for table decoration. The glass was often decorated with prunts, pinchings or flowers, in flint or coloured glass, and was sometimes decorated with gilding. The most common patterns for air trap decoration were a diamond-quilted pattern (sometimes known as 'Venetian diamond') herringbone, swirl, *moiré* and raindrop – a simple spot effect. Sometimes parts of the third outer layer were etched away to leave sprays of flowers in relief, rather in the manner of cameo glass. Such elaborations were produced by Thomas Webb's, following their patent of 1889. Various 'rainbow', striped and shaded effects were developed. One variety was Richardson's 'Tartan' glass registered in 1886, which had a plaid pattern. This pattern was achieved by laying rods of coloured glass on the body before it was fully formed. These variegated, coloured patterns in satin glass were facilitated by the 'pull-up' machine invented by John Northwood and patented in England in 1885. Previously, the glass-maker, after running his fine thread round the glass vessel from top to bottom, took a sharp, pointed hook and pulled the threads upwards, starting from the bottom. This was repeated many times round the vessel, transforming the horizontal threads into a series of festoons. This was a slow and laborious process and the result was often irregular. To overcome this difficulty, John Northwood developed a machine which consisted of a circular mould made of flat steel blades with the edges directed towards the centre, the inner edges being made like a saw with sharp points. Each alternative blade was fixed, the other movable, both attached at the base to a thread iron which, by means of a hand-wheel underneath, forced the blades upwards. The body of the vessel was covered with horizontal threads as before and, while still hot and pliable, was placed in the mould and blown until the

158 Bowl in layered glass with turquoise blue on the outside and furnace-wrought rustic and pincered decoration in clear colourless glass. This decoration was designed by John Northwood and registered under the title of 'Matsu-no-kee' in 1884. Made by Stevens & Williams *c.* 1884 with 'Rd.15353' etched on the base. *Private collection.*

surface threads pressed up against the saw-edged blades. A boy operated the hand-wheel and the movable blades pulled up the section of the threads that they engaged, while the fixed blades held the other section of threads in a fixed position. When the object came out of the mould the threads had a regular zigzag pattern. According to the placing of the blades, various herringbone and festoon patterns could be achieved quickly and accurately (Plate 155). The idea was soon copied by many continental factories.

Since not only the Stourbridge and Birmingham factories produced satin glass, but also many factories in Bohemia, France, and the United States, it is very difficult to attribute pieces to a particular glass-works. A number of signed pieces emanating from Thomas Webb's and Stevens & Williams are found, but these form the exception rather than the rule.

Many fancy glasses with marbled and streaked effects were developed in the 1880s. In present-day dealers' terms many of these are now loosely and inaccurately described as 'end-of-day' glass but contemporary references and illustrations show that specific names were given to each variety. Mills & Walker of Stourbridge, for example, produced a 'Carrara' ware in imitation of marble in 1888. This is illustrated in a Silber & Fleming catalogue of 1889 where the marbled effect is shown in blue, citron, ruby and cream. A similar ware with a marbled and streaked effect called 'Marmara' is illustrated in the same catalogue, but the manufacturer cannot be positively identified. Of the same type was the 'Balzarine' glass of Stone, Fawdry & Stone of Birmingham, which had horizontal streaks and was made in blue, pink, citron, and mixed colours, in the typical fancy shapes of the mid- and late 1880s.

A type of surface decoration known as 'coralene' was achieved by tiny pieces of beads of flint or coloured glass which were fired on to the surface, the pieces adhering to enamel that had been painted on in the desired pattern, the subsequent firing giving a firm fixing. Many of the patterns were in imitation of tiny branches of coral (hence the name) but other patterns are found. In 1886 Mills &

159 Bowl of ivory-coloured opaque glass moulded with channels to form an air twist beneath a pale ruby outer layer, with applied rusticated decoration and satin finish. Made by Stevens & Williams, Brierley Hill. *c.* 1885. h. 5½ in. *Borough of Stourbridge Collection.*

Walker of Stourbridge produced a coralene decorated glass which they called '*Verre de Neige*' or 'Snowflake' glass. The *Pottery Gazette* described this glass as one in which 'various coloured bodies are cased on the outer surface with a substance which gives, after careful manipulation, a very realistic effect of the crisp appearance of a surface over which snowflakes have just fallen'. This 'Snowflake' glass which was made into vases, baskets, epergnes and flower bowls in several colours, is illustrated in the Silber & Fleming catalogue for 1889. A ruby snowflake glass was also produced by Richardson's in 1887.

A more sophisticated type of fancy glass of an imitative nature was the 'Moss Agate' glass of Stevens & Williams (Plate 156) introduced by John Northwood about 1888 and designed by Fred Carder, then their Chief Designer, who later emigrated to the United States, joining the Corning Glass Company. This 'Moss Agate' glass, which is reminiscent of the effects achieved by the French glass artists Eugène Rousseau and his pupil Léveillé, gives a credible imitation of the actual mineral, giving an appearance of weight and solidity. Indeed, the weight of the glass approximates that of the true moss agate. The glass was built up in three layers, the inside crackled, then a layer with coloured mossy streaks, and an outer layer of clear flint. The glass was usually produced in simple shapes – bowls or vases with flint handles – of a severity that was in contrast to the fussy designs of much of the contemporary fancy glass. This classical simplicity was appreciated by the *Pottery Gazette*, which in October 1888, describing the 'Moss Agate' glass, stated that 'in museum shapes it looks very well'.

In the Stourbridge area, furnace manipulated applied decoration was widespread but much of the decoration was fairly haphazard with a variety of odd prunts, pinchings and trailings. Much of it was Venetian-inspired but the resulting fancy glass was very different from the sophisticated Venetian-style glass produced by Powell's of Whitefriars, which resulted from a scholarly approach to the historic prototypes. A number of more controlled designs were introduced, notably by Stevens & Williams, and often given specific names. One of the earliest was the 'Adams' style of decoration, introduced by Stevens & Williams in 1883. The body of the glass was peacock blue, ruby, citron or ivory, with applied festoons in crystal or coloured glass with ruby prunts. Some examples of this Adams style

160 Satin glass vase in blue and white with festoon decoration and crimped rim, the six feet made of one piece of pincered glass and the whole acid-finished. Made by W. H., B. & J. Richardson, Stourbridge. *c.* 1885. h. $6^1/_2$ in. *Victoria & Albert Museum.*

decoration are illustrated in the *Pottery Gazette* (June 1883, p. 561) and the decoration was applied to a wide variety of articles, including bowls, vases, jugs and goblets. This was followed in the same year by their 'Acanthus' glass which achieved a wide popularity and was imitated by other firms. The body of the glass was usually coloured with acanthus leaves in clear glass, sometimes with a matt or satin finish, the leaves curling round the body and the stems turned up to form feet. A variation of this style called 'Autumnal Glass' was advertised in colour by the dealers Blumberg & Company of Cannon Street, London, in the *Pottery Gazette* (1 May 1884). This may have been produced by John Walsh Walsh of Birmingham who advertised their 'Autumnal Ware' in a later issue. This firm were certainly producing glass with applied leaves and fish in clear

161 Satin glass vase with diamond air traps. Made by Stevens & Williams, Brierley Hill. *c.* 1885. *Borough of Stourbridge (Northwood Collection).*

glass on crushed strawberry and electric blue glass in 1883, illustrated in the November *Pottery Gazette* (Plate 157).

A more ambitious style of applied decoration was the 'Matsu-no-kee' glass of Stevens & Williams, registered on 18 October 1884 and designed by John Northwood. Here rustic stems in crystal glass with daisy-like flowers in a Japanese style were applied to a coloured glass vessel. A patent spring pincer for the shaping of the blossoms and a spring stamping device for impressing flower patterns was invented by John Northwood which greatly simplified the production of these elaborate pieces. Most pieces of 'Matsu-no-kee' have 'Rd.15353' etched or engraved somewhere on the body and the bowl illustrated in Plate 158 is a typical marked example. Other varieties of this applied naturalistic decoration were produced at Stevens & Williams (Plate 159), including blackthorn sprays and rustic twigs without flowers, on various types of coloured glass including *'Verre-de-Soie'* (satin glass), glass with 'pull-up' patterns and threaded glass.

A close copy of Stevens & Williams' 'Matsu-no-kee' was produced by Richardson's in 1885 with flint daisies on rustic stems. Vases were also made with applied prunus blossom flower heads. Many other Stourbridge firms produced similar glass with naturalistic applied decoration. In December 1884 Mills and Walker registered designs for applied decoration including one of oak leaves and acorn while Stuart & Sons of the Red House Glass Works, Stourbridge produced their 'Iris' leaf and flower decoration in 1885. John Walsh Walsh of Birmingham produced their 'Flora' glass, decorated with daisies and convolvulus in 1884 and their 'Honeysuckle' glass, with applied sprays of the blossom and leaf, was registered in October 1885.

In 1885 Thomas Webb produced a whole series of fancy glass with applied fruit and flowers, often of an astonishing complexity. One bowl with a crimped top had a yellow body with applied topaz leaves and fruit for feet, another had a topaz body, lined with ivory glass, with olive green leaves, topaz fruit which was then silvered, the body being blown in a honeycomb mould. An even more elaborate example, a vase some eleven inches high, had a topaz body shaped with pink at the top, olive green shell and scrolled feet, applied stems of olive green with topaz leaves shading to brown embellished with pink flowers and birds. Webb's produced vases in the shape of melons, marrows and gourds, all with applied decorations, as well as glass apples and pears for table decorations, paperweights and menu-holders. Similar fancy glass by Thomas Webb with applied fish and reptiles has been described in detail in the chapter on painted and enamelled glass.

These fancy glasses of Thomas Webb's were paralleled by those of

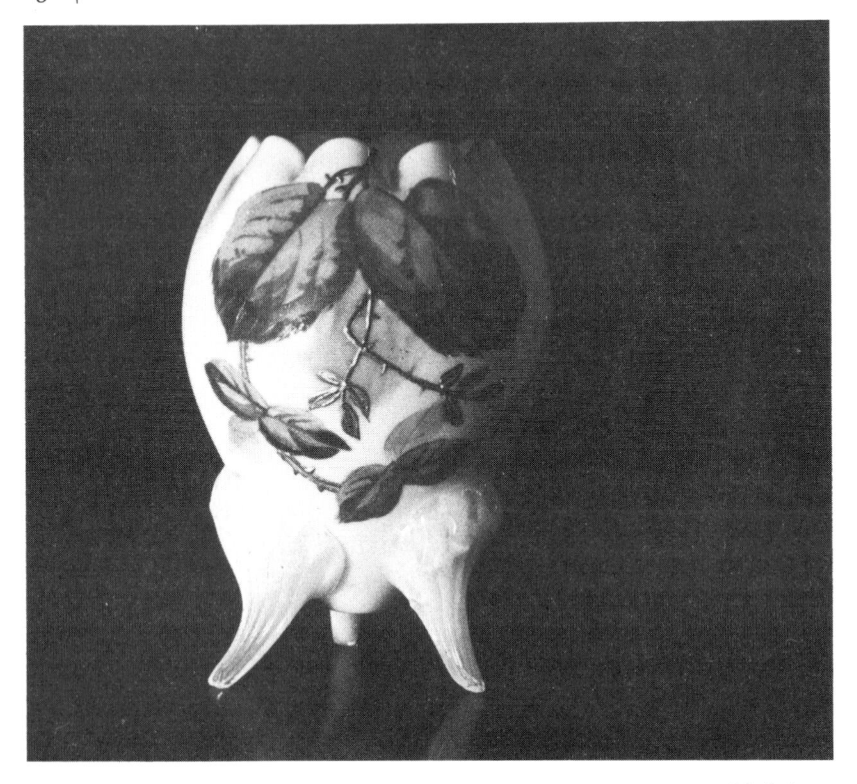

162 Satin glass vase with applied ribbed feet and painted and gilded decoration. Made by Edward Webb, White House Glass Works, Wordsley. *c.* 1885. h. $3^1/_2$ in. *Brierley Hill Collection.*

Richardson's. Indeed, at this period, whatever one Stourbridge glass-works did, the other glass-works copied and in the absence of any marks, it is difficult to make a precise attribution.

In 1879 Richardson's revised the applied snakes that they had employed in the mid-century, curling them round the neck of a decanter, or the stem of a wine glass, or round the body of the vase. In November of that year, they produced a range of vases in flint glass decorated with blobs of blue, green and ruby glass, shaped like tadpoles. An applied fish foot, with open mouth, was registered by Richardson's in November 1881, the inside of the mouth being sometimes gilt. Much use was made of applied flint fish, newts and insects, as well as applied leaf and flower ornament, sometimes simply in flint, sometimes in naturalistic colours with the leaves in green or amber and the flowers in ruby or magenta. This naturalistic decoration was applied to centrepieces as well as to vases. In May 1883 Richardson's produced vases, similar to those of Thomas Webb, with amber glass pears and leaves in 'Connemara' green on a ruby body with flint feet.

In the 1880s, a number of shaded fancy glasses were produced more or less simultaneously in the Stourbridge area and in the United States, in some instances the patent being first taken out in the United States, with the right to manufacture under licence subsequently passing to an English firm. One such glass was 'Amberina', first patented by the New English Glass Company of Boston on 21 July 1883. It was the invention of an Englishman, Joseph Locke, the son of a potter at the Royal Worcester Porcelain factory, who was born on 21 August 1846. At the age of twelve, Joseph Locke joined the Worcester factory as an apprentice, leaving it at the age of nineteen to join Guest Brothers, glass decorators of Stourbridge. A few years later he moved to Hodgetts, Richardson & Son, where he was instrumental in the development of cameo glass (see Chapter 6). After brief connections with Philip Pargeter and Thomas Webb he left England in 1882 for the United States, where he was immediately engaged by the New England Glass Company. 'Amberina' was the first of his many patents for that firm. In the patent it was described as 'a novel class of glassware . . . being composed of homogeneous stock, having different or contrasting colours blended or merged one into another . . . the glass for the production of the entire article is all the result of the same mixture and is taken from the same pot, the changes in colour being produced entirely in the manufacture of the ware by the action upon it of varying degrees of heat'. As its name implies, 'Amberina' was basically an amber coloured glass shading to deep ruby. A licence to produce pressed 'Amberina' was granted to Sowerby's Ellison Glass Works. In March 1884 the *Pottery Gazette* described the 'Amberina' glass being sold by Messrs Blumberg & Co. of Cannon Street. The glass, which was made in a variety of fancy shapes, was deep ruby at the top, gradually merging into amber at the bottom, without any particular line of demarcation as to where one colour begins and the other ends. The interior of the glass had a flattened, ball-like surface which reflected the light through, as the glass was transparent, unlike similar shaded glasses which will be described later. As Blumberg & Co. were merchants or retailers (with an establishment in Paris as well as London) and not glass manufacturers it is by no means certain that their 'Amberina' was of English origin, for most factories throughout Europe and the United States produced some specimens of 'Amberina' during the 1880s and later. Another fancy glass that was evidently similar to 'Amberina' was the 'Sunrise' glass of Burtles, Tate & Company of the Victoria Glass Works, Bolton, introduced in 1892. The sunrise effect was produced by a skilful shading of opalescent glass, deepening gradually from yellow or amber to pink with ruby edges.

On 13 July 1886, a further patent was granted to Joseph Locke for a variation of 'Amberina', known as 'Plated Amberina', whereby the glass was given a creamy opal lining. This was very similar to the 'Peach Glass' of Thomas Webb and the 'Peach Blow' of several American companies.

Webb's 'Peach Glass', perfected in 1885, was described by the *Pottery Gazette* as a 'delicate blend of colour shaded so as to imitate a peach'. It consisted of two layers, the outer layer shading from pink at the base to deep red at the top, the inner layer of cream with a slightly greenish tinge. The outer surface was left either glossy or acidised, to give a semi-matt, peach-like bloom. It was mostly used for vases and ornaments and was frequently enriched with gilding or applied crystal decoration. A similar 'Peach Blow' was produced by Stevens & Williams. According to a report in the *New York Mail*, quoted by the *Pottery Gazette* (2 August 1886), a veritable craze for 'Peach Blow' had developed. Under the heading 'The Craze for Peach Blows' the report stated that the real name for the colour was crushed strawberry, 'but people who are crazy for it call it "peach blow" and that makes it so'. A glass with an apricot-tinged outer layer and a cream lining had indeed been advertised in colour by John Walsh Walsh of Birmingham under the name of 'Crushed Strawberry' in the *Pottery Gazette* as early as November 1883. The illustration shows a number of vases, mostly with applied crystal decoration in the form of acanthus leaves, shells and fish, with additional prunts, including one at the base to obscure the pontil mark.

Richardson's do not appear to have introduced 'Amberina' until 1894. From then on they produced a number of water sets in this glass, in ribbed and festoon moulded patterns, as well as vases and centrepieces. Some of the vases were ribbed and twisted, diamond or

163 Two 'Ivory Cameo' vases, the opaque white glass bodies tinted and acid-finished to resemble ivory, with acid-etched relief decoration. Made by Thomas Webb, Stourbridge, the provisional patent specification for this glass in imitation of 'old carved ivory' being entered on 30 November 1887. The bases are marked 'Thos Webb & Sons'. h. 12½ in. and 9 in. *Sotheby's Belgravia.*

wave moulded, or 'blabbed', often with hollow twist or knopped stems. Others are tall, trumpet-shaped vases with a band of cut decoration below a blocked or waved top. A registered pattern (no. 261066) of a lyre-shaped flower holder, complete with glass strings was produced in 'Amberina' as well as in other colours and flint.

One of the most popular and most commercially successful among the novelties of the later 1880s was Thomas Webb's 'Burmese' glass, patented under the name of 'Queen's Burmese Ware'. It is an opaque, single-layered glass which shades from a pale greenish yellow to a deep salmon pink. It was first patented in the United States by Frederick Shirley on behalf of the Mount Washington Glass Company, New Bedford, Massachusetts, on 15 December 1885. To a well-known mixture for transluscent white or opal glass was added oxide of uranium and a small amount of prepared gold. The uranium oxide made the ordinarily transluscent white melt to a pale, solid yellow and the small amount of gold, made soluble in *aqua regia*, was dispersed colloidally throughout the whole batch. This

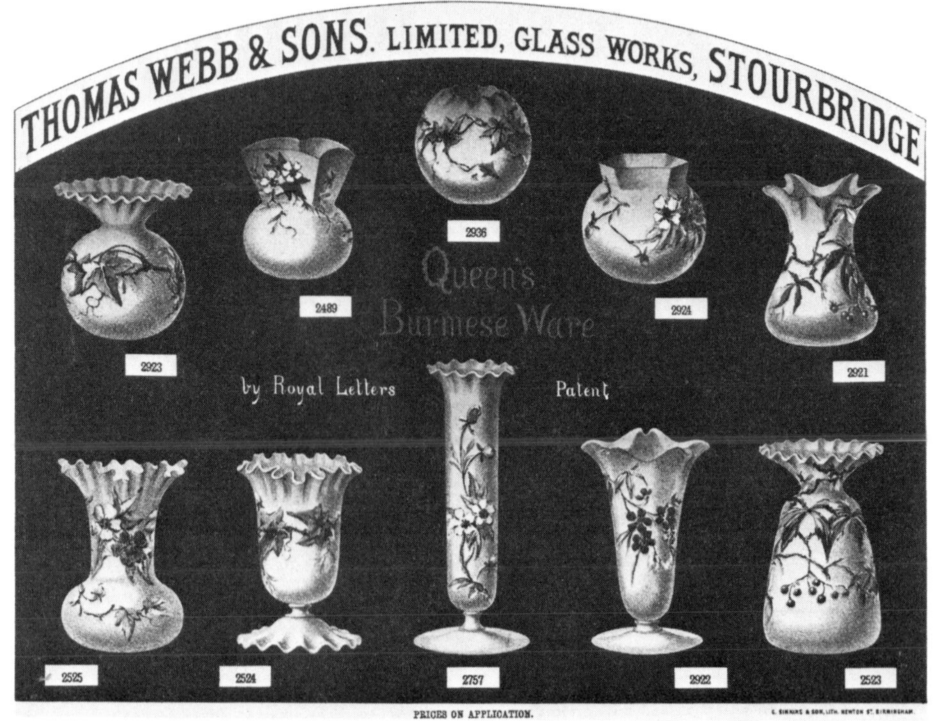

164 Advertisement from the *Pottery Gazette* of 1887 for Thomas Webb's patent 'Queen's Burmese Ware'. *Colour lithograph.*

made the glass sensitive to thermal changes. After the article was formed – either free or mould blown – it was allowed to cool below a glowing red heat. A portion of the glass was then reheated at the glory-hole and the reheated portion then turned salmon pink, shading down to the original pale yellow.

On 16 June 1886, Shirley's formula for Burmese glass was patented in England and the sole right to production in England was acquired by Thomas Webb. Webb's called this new fancy glass 'Queen's Burmese Ware' as the first service, a set of coffee cups and saucers enamelled with daisies, was presented to Queen Victoria. Thomas Webb had the right to copy the Mount Washington designs as well as produce their own shapes and decoration, and to export them to Europe and the United States. Most of the Webb Burmese glass was acid finished, giving it a matt surface, but the Mount Washington product was sometimes left glossy.

From the onset Burmese glass was used extensively for the new patent 'Fairy Lights' which had just come into being, and for small individual candle shades. The individual fairy lights were often made up into large hanging chandeliers or set on plateaux to form table decorations. Sometimes the fairy lights were combined with flower vases and holders (Plate 165). Many of these candelabra and centrepieces are illustrated in colour in the *Pottery Gazette* (1887 and 1888) but few have survived intact.

'Queen's Burmese Ware' was particularly popular for small flower vases, of varying shapes, often with a crimped top, and sometimes also a crimped foot (Plate 164)). An attractive petal shaped top, registered by Thomas Webb on 5 August, was also extensively used. A Thomas Webb pattern book of drawings for Burmese glass, dating from 1886 to 1887, shows that it was also used for large water jugs, tumblers and goblets, but the smaller items accounted for most of their production in this field.

Some of the pieces were left plain but enamelled decoration was common, for once the shaded tint had been achieved, a return to the furnace did not alter the colour. Most of the enamelled decoration was naturalistic, consisting of trailing ivy leaves, leaves and berries, various types of blossom, and chrysanthemums.

The largest was undoubtedly a five-hundred light 'Fairy Pyramid' chandelier in 'Queen's Burmese Ware' which is illustrated in the *Pottery Gazette* (1888) as being in the course of construction. It

165 Table centrepiece of Thomas Webb's 'Queen's Burmese Ware', painted in enamel colours, made to hold Clarke's Patent Fairy Lights, the metal fittings stamped 'SAMUEL CLARKE'. The same design, without the painted decoration, was illustrated in the *Pottery Gazette*, 1 April 1887. Overall h. 8 in. *Sotheby's Belgravia*.

was made to hang in the centre dome of the Conservatory in the Royal Botanic Society's Garden in Regent's Park, London, for their fête on 4 July 1888. It was twelve feet long and weighed five hundredweights. It does not appear to have survived, for most of these special Fairy Light illuminations were assembled expressly for festive occasions, including various Jubilee celebrations, and dismantled after the event.

The current Japanese influence was reflected in the assymetrical placing of the sprays and in the choice of almond blossom and chrysanthemums. Other Burmese vases were decorated with landscapes with figures of warriors and 'Kate Greenaway' type children. Several designs for vases in Burmese glass were produced for the 1887 Golden Jubilee. These were decorated with freely trailing sprays of roses, thistles and shamrock and a ribbon inscribed '1837 Jubilee 1887'. The enamelling of these Burmese items was carried out under the direction of Jules Barbe.

In the late 1880s the demand for the 'Queen's Burmese Ware' exceeded the supply but it was a fashion of fairly short duration which gradually petered out in the 1890s.

The 'Uranium' glass of Burtles, Tate & Company, which preceded their 'Sunrise' glass, was probably so named on account of a uranium content and as such was probably similar to the 'Queen's Burmese Ware' of Thomas Webb.

Another type of glass that was produced on much the same principle as Burmese glass was 'Alexandrite', first advertised by Stevens & Williams in July 1887 and also produced by Thomas Webb about the same time. It was a single layered transparent glass, blown either plain or in a rippled or diamond patterned mould, which shaded from amber through a rose or fuschia colour to blue. The colour change was achieved by reheating at the furnace. It was especially popular for wine glasses and finger bowls. 'Alexandrite' was also made in the United States and at Ludwig Moser's factory at Karlsbad (now Karlovy Vary) in Bohemia.

Towards the end of the century, the art nouveau style was manifest in a number of varieties of fancy glass, not only in the shapes of the vessels themselves, but also in the choice of decoration. Many Stourbridge firms produced clear glass vases, rose bowls, centrepieces and decanters which were decorated with blobs and trails of green glass. A characteristic range, called the 'Peacock' is illustrated in a Harrods catalogue of about 1900. The decoration consists of the 'eye' of a peacock's feather in two shades of green with a trail of green glass placed at intervals round the vessel. The vases have waved or turned-over rims, and some have metal mounts. Similar glass appears in Liberty's catalogues of the same date, some decorated with green glass, others with blobs of crystal glass.

The turn of the century also saw a revival of straw opal or yellow opal glass. Some of it was in Venetian shapes, including fan and trumpet vases, similar to those produced by James Powell & Sons in the late 1870s, but much of it was in a marked art nouveau style. A new development was mould blown glass vases in straw or yellow opaline with the patterns showing opaque against a clear background. The Richardson pattern books from 1898 onwards show a number of these vases with scrolled designs or swirling patterns of flowers and leaves. The later ones are described as being blown in an electric mould. This mould blown opaline glass was also much used for gas and electric light shades and for centrepieces, particularly those in floral forms (see Chapter 9).

APPENDIX 1

REGISTRY MARKS

Glass objects (particularly pressed glass objects) made between 1842 and 1883 sometimes bear a diamond shaped mark which indicates that they were registered at the Patent Office Design Registry. The mark can be used to determine the exact date of registration and, by consulting official records held by the Public Record Office, the name of the firm or person registering the design. Glass objects were registered under Class III.

After 1883 a new series of registrations began which are indicated on the object by a serial number. These numerical registrations were not divided into classes but continued in straight sequence irrespective of material. Details of the numbers of the first registration in each year from 1884 to 1901 are given below.

(*a*) 1842 to 1867

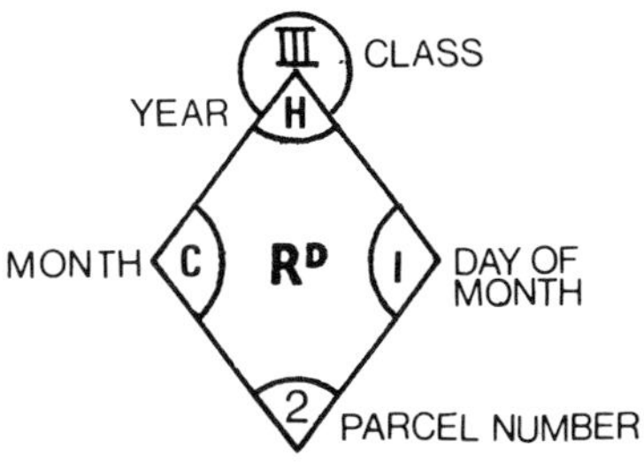

CLASS (III)
YEAR (H)
MONTH (C)
Rd
DAY OF MONTH (1)
PARCEL NUMBER (2)

1 January 1843

Years		*Months*	
1842 — X	1855 — E	January	— C
1843 — H	1856 — L	February	— G
1844 — C	1857 — K	March	— W
1845 — A	1858 — B	April	— H
1846 — I	1859 — M	May	— E
1847 — F	1860 — Z	June	— M
1848 — U	1861 — R	July	— I
1849 — S	1862 — O	August	— R
1850 — V	1863 — G	September	— D
1851 — P	1864 — N	October	— B
1852 — D	1865 — W	November	— K
1853 — Y	1866 — Q	December	— A
1854 — J	1867 — T		

(R may be found as the month mark for 1–19 September 1857, and K for December 1860.)

(*b*) 1868 to 1883

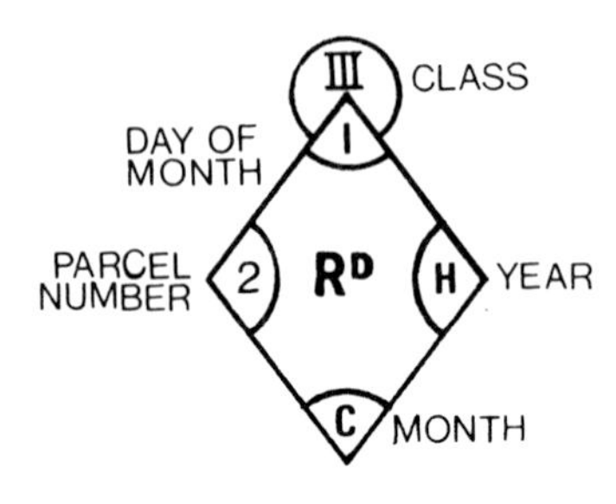

1st January 1869

Years		*Months*	
1868—X	1876—V	January	—C
1869—H	1877—P	February	—G
1870—C	1878—D	March	—W
1871—A	1879—Y	April	—H
1872—I	1880—J	May	—E
1873—F	1881—E	June	—M
1874—U	1882—L	July	—I
1875—S	1883—K	August	—R
		September	—D
		October	—B
		November	—K
		December	—A

(For 1–6 March 1878, G was used for the month and W for the year.)

(*c*) 1884 to 1901

1884— 1	1890—141273	1896—268392
1885— 19754	1891—163767	1897—291241
1886— 40480	1892—185713	1898—311658
1887— 64520	1893—205240	1899—331707
1888— 90483	1894—224720	1900—351202
1889—116648	1895—246975	1901—368154

APPENDIX 2

TRADE OR FACTORY MARKS

Marks on hand-made glass are rare apart from signatures of engravers, printed or painted marks on the base of vases, such as those by Richardson's and Bacchus & Co. in the mid-nineteenth century. The following marks appear on pressed glass in the latter part of the nineteenth century, and on some pieces of Thomas Webb's glass from 1890 onwards.

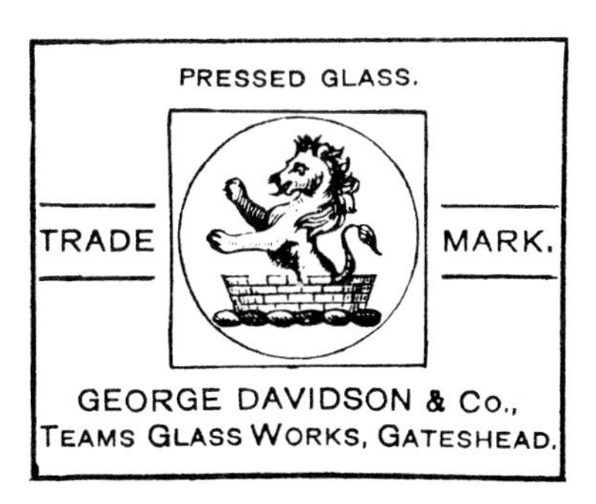

Greener & Co., Wear Glass Works,
Sunderland

Trade mark of John Derbyshire & Company,
Regent Road Flint Glass Works, Manchester.

SELECTED BIBLIOGRAPHY

Contemporary Works

PELLATT, Apsley. *Curiosities of Glassmaking*. London, 1849.
RUSKIN, John. *The Stones of Venice*, London, 1851–3.
EASTLAKE, Charles Lock. *Hints on Household Taste*, 1868.
DRESSER, Christopher. *Principles of Decorative Design*,
REDGRAVE, Richard. *Manual of Design* (South Kensington Museum Art Handbook) 1876.
BREMNER, David. *Industries of Scotland*, Edinburgh, 1869.

Periodicals
Art Union 1839–1848.
Art Journal 1849–1912.
Journal of Design and Manufactures 1849–1851.
Pottery Gazette and Glass Trades Review, 1877–
The Studio 1893–

Contemporary International Exhibition Catalogues

Great Exhibition of the Industry of All Nations, London, 1851.
Dublin International Exhibition, 1853.
Universal Exhibition, Paris, 1855.
International Exhibition, London, 1862.
Universal Exhibition, Paris, 1867.
International Exhibition, London, 1871.
Universal Exhibition, Vienna, 1873.

Philadelphia Centennial Exhibition, 1876.
Universal Exhibition, Paris, 1878.
Universal Exhibition, Paris, 1889.

Modern Works

BEARD, Geoffrey W. *Nineteenth Century Cameo Glass*, Newport, 1956.

CROMPTON, Sidney. *English Glass*, London, 1967.

GODDEN, Geoffrey A. *Antique China and Glass under £5*, London, 1966.

GUTTERY, D. R. *From Broad-Glass to Cut Crystal*, London, 1956.

HOLLISTER, Paul. *The Encyclopaedia of Glass Paperweights*, New York, 1969.

HONEY, W. B. *English Glass*, London, 1946.

JOKELSON, Paul. *Sulphides. The Art of Cameo Incrustation*, New York, 1968.

POLAK, Ada. *Glass: its makers and its public*, London, 1975.

POWELL, Harry J. *Glass-making in England*, Cambridge, 1923.

NORTHWOOD, John Jn. *John Northwood*, Stourbridge, 1958.

THORPE, W. A. *English Glass*, London, 1935.

WAKEFIELD, Hugh. *19th Century British Glass*, London, 1961.

WEBBER, Norman W. *Collecting Glass*, Newton Abbot, 1972.

WESTROPP, M. A. Dudley, *Irish Glass*, London, 1920 (reprinted 1978).

Recent Exhibition Catalogues

Exhibition of Victorian and Edwardian Decorative Arts, Victoria & Albert Museum, London, 1952.

The Handley Read Collection. Royal Academy London, 1972.

English 'Rock Crystal' Glass 1878–1925. Dudley Art Gallery, 1976.

INDEX